DUDE
CRAFTS

Brimming with creative inspiration, how-to projects, and useful information to enrich your everyday life, Quarto Knows is a favorite destination for those pursuing their interests and passions. Visit our site and dig deeper with our books into your area of interest: Quarto Creates, Quarto Cooks, Quarto Homes, Quarto Lives, Quarto Drives, Quarto Explores, Quarto Gifts, or Quarto Kids.

First published in 2018 by Voyageur Press, an imprint of The Quarto Group,
401 Second Avenue North, Suite 310, Minneapolis, MN 55401 USA.
T (612) 344-8100 F (612) 344-8692
www.QuartoKnows.com

Voyageur Press titles are also available at discount for retail, wholesale, promotional, and bulk purchase. For details, contact the Special Sales Manager by email at specialsales@quarto.com or by mail at The Quarto Group, Attn: Special Sales Manager, 401 Second Avenue North, Suite 310, Minneapolis, MN 55401 USA.

10 9 8 7 6 5 4 3 2 1

ISBN: 978-0-7603-5778-1

Library of Congress Cataloging-in-Publication Data

Names: Warren, Mike, 1980- author.
Title: Dude crafts : the man's guide to practical projects, backyard ballistics, and glorious gags / Mike Warren.
Description: Minneapolis, MN : Voyageur Press, an imprint of The Quarto Group, 2018.
Identifiers: LCCN 2018016682 | ISBN 9780760357781 (sc)
Subjects: LCSH: Handicraft. | Amusements. | Practical jokes.
Classification: LCC TT157 .W3566 2018 | DDC 745.5--dc23
LC record available at https://lccn.loc.gov/2018016682

Acquiring Editor: Dennis Pernu
Project Manager: Alyssa Lochner
Art Director: James Kegley
Cover Designer: Amelia LeBarron
Layout: Amelia LeBarron

Printed in China

For safety, use caution, care, and good judgment when following the procedures described in this book. The publisher and author cannot assume responsibility for any damage to property or injury to persons as a result of misuse of the information provided. Further, the projects in this book vary widely as to skill levels required: some may not be appropriate for all do-it-yourselfers.

DUDE CRAFTS

THE MAN'S GUIDE TO PRACTICAL PROJECTS, BACKYARD BALLISTICS, AND GLORIOUS GAGS

MIKE WARREN

VOYAGEUR PRESS

CONTENTS

STYLISH LIVING

INTRODUCTION

It's time to bring those half-baked ideas that were dreamed up on the toilet to life. Whether you're making your life easier through clever inventions or bringing to life a concept that's been hiding in your mind, this book is here to help get your creative wheels turning.

The functional (and sometime dangerous) projects in these pages represent a cross section that any "dude" worth his salt would find helpful. Whether in the man cave, workshop, or on the streets, dude-craft projects are designed to get you comfortable making while having fun doing it.

The step-by-step projects shown here approach making from a functional standpoint, and don't require any specialized tools or knowledge to get started. For those up for more of a challenge, there are a few projects that will test your maker mettle. Some of the projects I make throw caution to the wind in the spirit of uncovering new ideas. As such, only attempt projects within your ability and comfort zone. I'm all for stretching your knowledge and learning new things, but it's never worth it if you end up hurt. The projects in this book are meant to inspire and entertain, and are not authoritative instructions for safe methods. Be smart about what you read and attempt.

My goal for this book is to give you the tools needed to be comfortable making. Once you've got the basics of this book down, my hope is that you'll have the confidence and momentum to continue making, either by remixing the projects in this book or by breaking all the rules and making your own creations.

Get ready to flex your maker muscles and let the world know you're an apex inventor.

-DUDE CRAFTS-
FINE
FOOD &
SPIRITS

BABY FLASK

MATERIALS AND TOOLS

- BABY-DOLL TOY
- DRILL
- SCISSORS
- HYDRATION PACK WITH BITE-STYLE DRINKING STRAW
- FRONT-HARNESS BABY CARRIER
- A NEED TO DRINK IN PUBLIC

Whether you're looking to sneak a beverage into a sports arena or just bring a beer to the movies, a fake baby is the perfect place to hide your hooch. Not only does looking like a parent elevate you to the status of "responsible person" in the eyes of others, but claiming your baby needs sleep and can't be bothered becomes a ready excuse to shoo away anyone who seems suspicious. (This buys you just enough time to make a hasty retreat before they get wise.) A baby flask for hiding your booze—what a time to be alive!

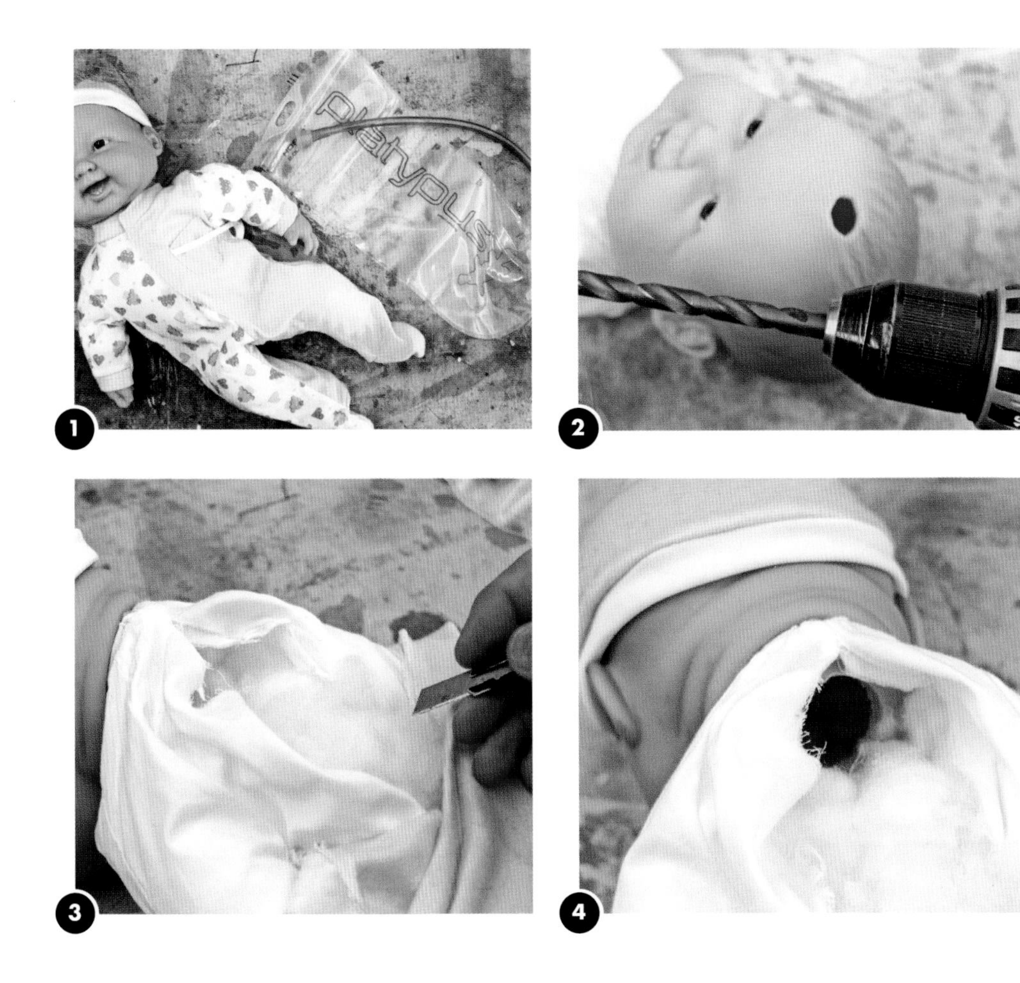

1. This build is simple, but the execution has a huge payoff. First, find an inexpensive baby doll with a plastic head and a soft fabric body. Then, find a soft plastic hydration system with a bite-valve drinking straw, such as those used for hiking and commonly found in sporting goods stores.

2. Drill an opening in the center of the doll's forehead to accommodate the bite valve. It's a good idea to undersize this opening so the valve is a tight fit.

3. Cut open the back of the baby doll and remove some of the stuffing.

4. There should be a clear opening through the neck and into the hollow cavity of the head, revealing the opening you just drilled. Detach the bite valve and feed the straw into the head and out the drilled opening, followed by the pouch, which is placed in the doll body.

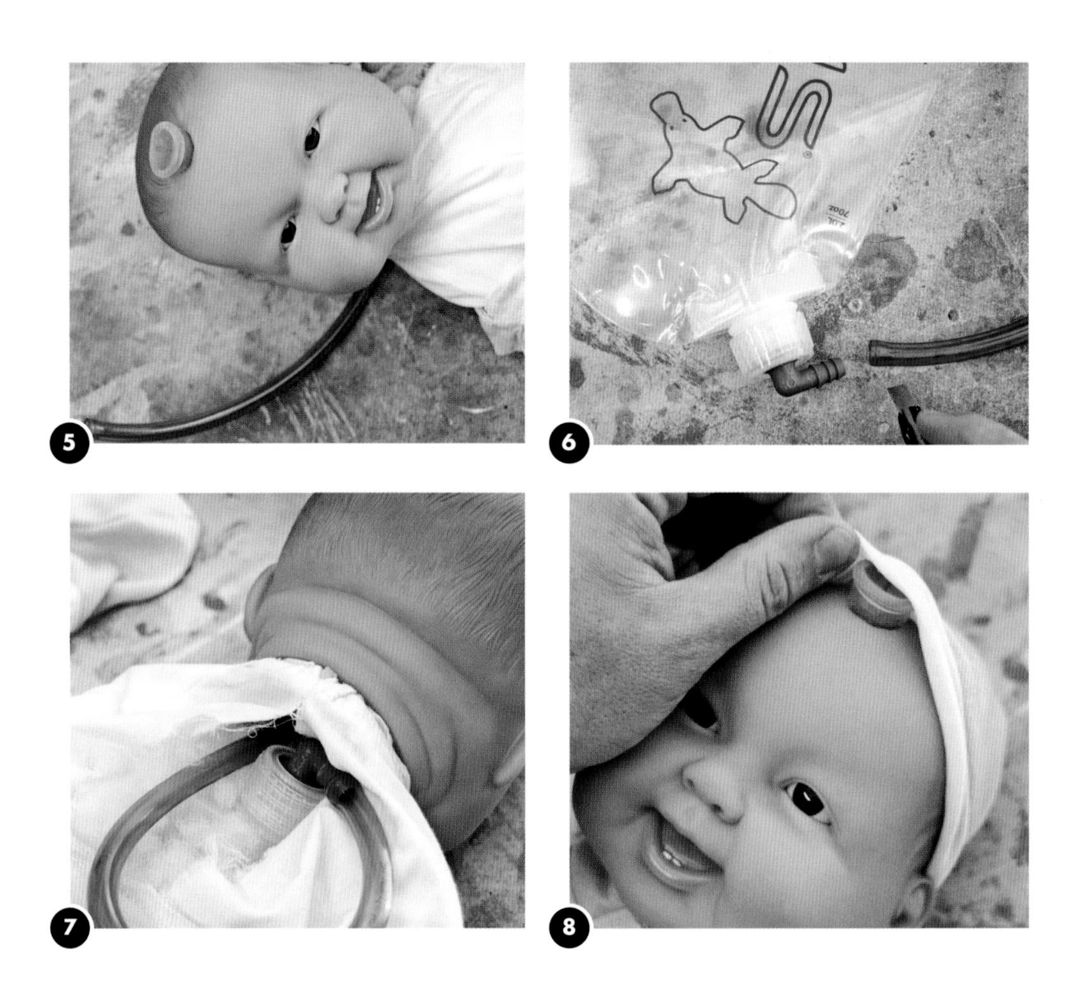

5. Push the bite valve into the drilled opening to make a snug fit.

6. Cut the hose to length and reattach to the pouch.

7. Work the pouch into the body of the doll to conceal it and reattach the hose to the bite valve inside the doll's head. Re-dress the doll to cover the cut backing.

8. The baby flask is complete! To fill, just lie the baby face down and open the back to access the hydration pack. Fill with your favorite beverage and seal shut. Carry your baby flask in a front-harness carrier with the doll facing you. You can easily hide the drinking bite with a baby cap. If you ever hear the sentences "What a cute baby!" and "Why does it smell like whiskey?" together, it might be time for a new project.

BBQ BRANDING IRON

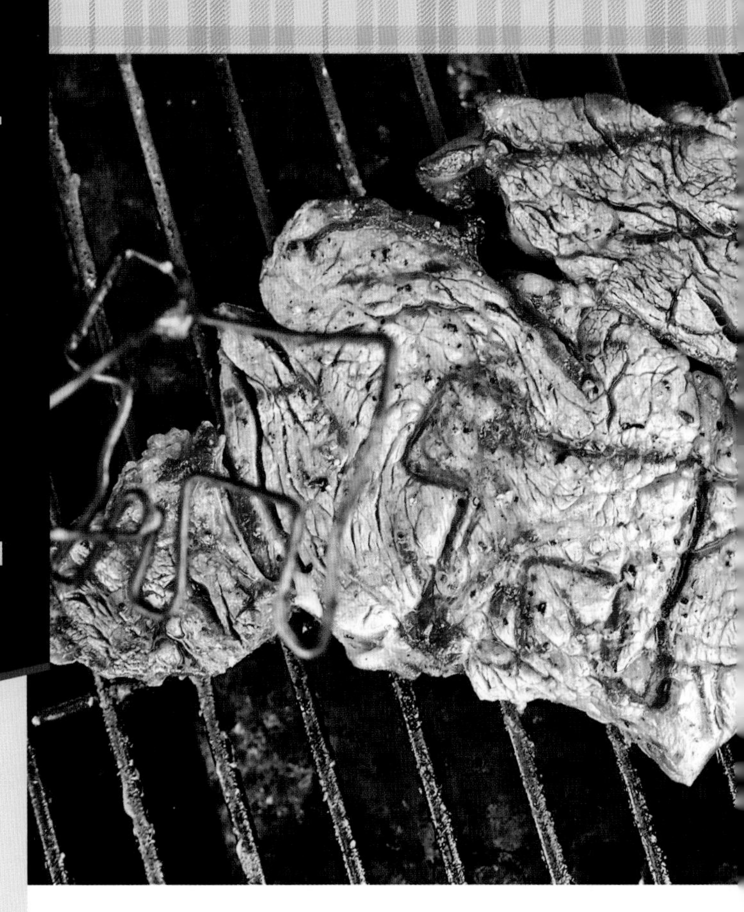

MATERIALS AND TOOLS

- OLD BICYCLE WHEEL
- HEAVY-DUTY SCOURING PAD
- PLIERS
- FLATHEAD SCREWDRIVER
- WIRE CUTTER
- PRINTER PAPER
- WELDER
- GRINDER

For me, there's nothing better than grilling outdoors. Sometimes when I'm staring into the fiery element, watching steaks cook, I wonder whether there's any way this could get better. Then, it hits me . . . personalized steaks! Branding steaks is a great way to make your next cookout unique. If you make a few different branding irons, you can mark your meats however you like!

To make your own BBQ branding irons, all you need are a few stainless-steel bicycle spokes. It might be tempting to make a custom branding iron from a wire coat hanger, but don't do it! These coat hangers are made from a metal alloy that might contain lead or other toxic metals. Stainless steel is food safe and really the only option for this project.

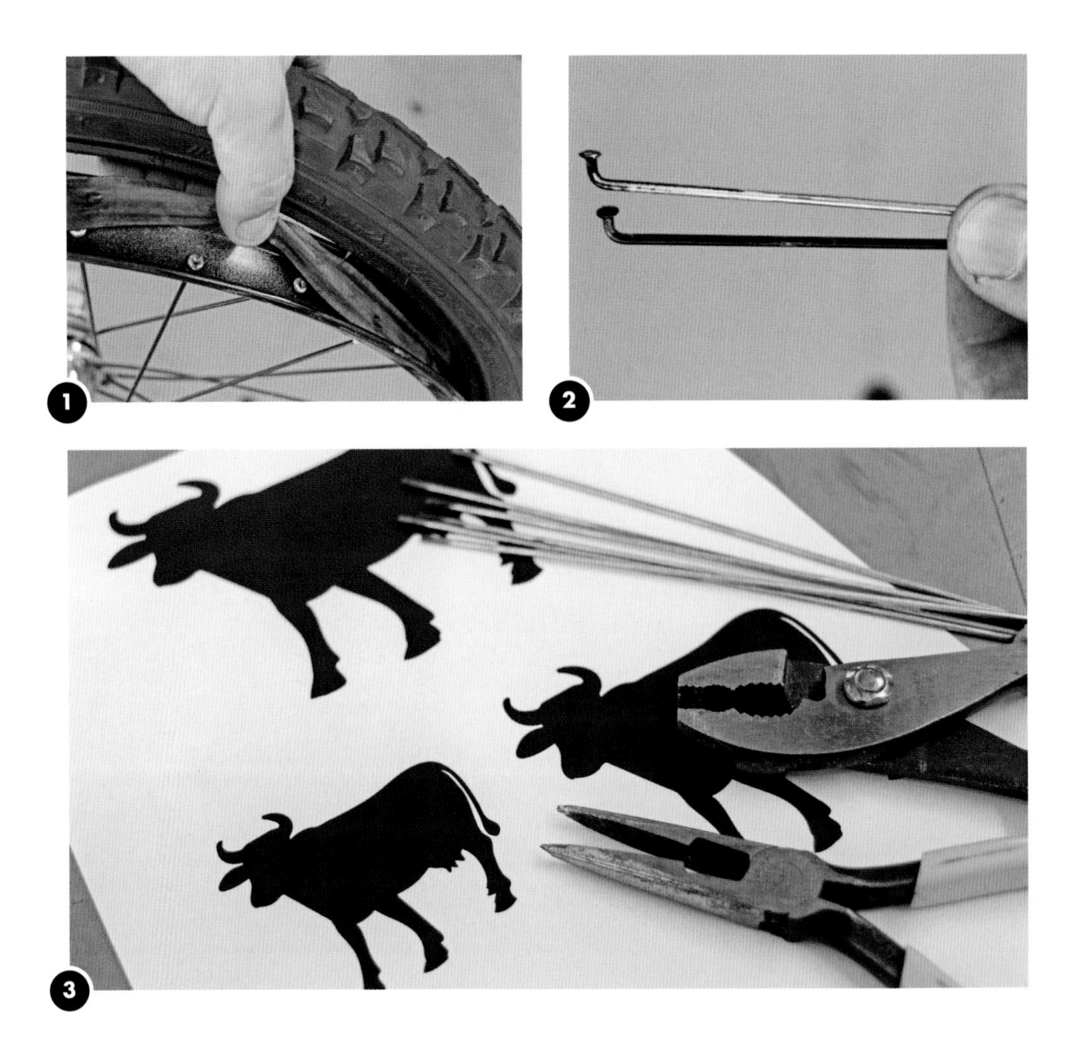

1. I started by dismantling a discarded bicycle wheel. You can find these at any bike shop; just make sure the spokes are stainless steel. Deflate and remove the tire from the rim, then remove the rubber rim strip that protects the inner tube from the nuts holding the spokes. The nuts are usually unthreaded and removed with a flathead screwdriver; then the spokes can be removed through the hub.

2. It's a good idea to clean the spokes with warm soapy water and a very rough scouring pad. This will remove any grease, grime, and other road detritus.

3. Now the fun part! Decide what shape you want the brand to be. You can find a shape template by searching for silhouettes online. This image was printed in a few different sizes on regular printer paper.

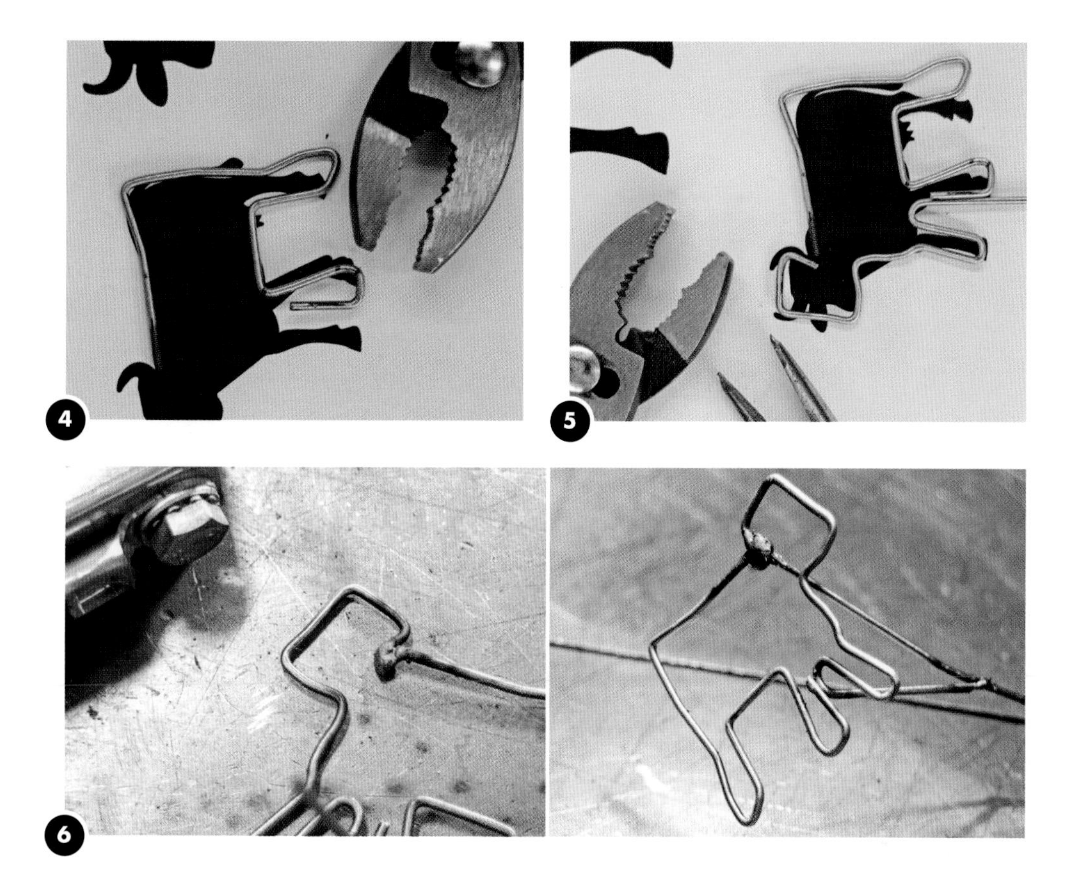

4. Determine the size that best works for you, and with your pliers bend a spoke around the printed shape.

5. Because one spoke probably won't be long enough for the entire outline of your shape, create your outline in sections that will be easily joined together later. Finish bending the shapes with pliers and then bend another spoke to act as a handle.

6. Use a welder to combine the shapes into a complete brand. This might sound difficult if you've never welded before, but this is a great project with which to get started welding since there are no points requiring super-tidy welds. Once you finish the welding, hit any high spots of the welds with a grinder to smooth out the rough edges, then use a scouring pad to refine any edges.

To use the brand, fire up your grill and bury the brand into the heat source until it's red hot. When your meat is on the grill, pull out the brand and plant it firmly into the steak to transfer the image. The heat dissipates quickly from the steel, so after each use bury the brand into the heat source before branding again.

BEER ADVENT CALENDAR

MATERIALS AND TOOLS

- **SHIPPING TUBES**
- **SAW**
- **SANDPAPER**
- **CARDBOARD**
- **HOT-GLUE GUN**
- **WRAPPING PAPER**

Cardboard shipping tubes used to mail posters and blueprints also happen to be just the right size to hold a standard beverage can. And they're long enough to be cut in several sections. Why not upcycle those old tubes in a fashion that will help spread Yuletide cheer?

1A and 1B. Use a saw to cut tubes into sections, each the same height (slightly taller than a can). Since this is an Advent calendar, you will need twenty-five sections.

2. Smooth out the cut edges of the tube sections with sandpaper.

3. Place the tube sections side by side, then use hot glue to join the sides of two tube sections.

4. Continue joining tube sections together on all sides until you have a rectangular honeycomb structure.

5. Cut a flat piece of cardboard to the size of the honeycomb structure. This will serve as the back side of the Advent calendar and prevent the cans from falling out the back.

6

7

8

9

6. Use more hot glue in select areas to join the cardboard back to the tubes.

7. Cut more flat cardboard to make a frame around the perimeter to neatly enclose the tubes, using hot glue to hold everything in place.

8. Fill each open tube with a canned beverage of your choice. I chose a mix of different styles of beer.

9. Once it's full, cover with wrapping paper and use clear tape to secure. Gently feel around the front of the box to determine the position of each can opening, then label each opening with a number from 1 to 25, in any order you like.

The last step before gifting this boozy present is to make a small incision at each numbered spot to make opening the event easier. And remember: the wrapping paper will be toast by Christmas Day, but the tube-and-cardboard structure can be rewrapped and used again year after year.

BOTTLE BANDOLIER

MATERIALS AND TOOLS

- OLD JEANS
- SEAM RIPPER
- FABRIC SCISSORS
- NEEDLE AND THREAD
- PINS
- NYLON STRAPPING
- LIGHTER (OPTIONAL)
- PLASTIC SIDE-SQUEEZE BUCKLE

Not all heroes wear capes—some wear combat bandoliers. Go prepared to your next patio party with a bandolier full of cold ones. That's right . . . the bottle bandolier will allow you to stay out and party without leaving to get a refill. Although this project involves sewing, it's dead simple and requires no fancy tricks.

This fashion statement will also bring the party to you, as you'll have enough refreshments to keep your friends happy too. The bottle bandolier has room to hold six cans of your favorite beverage and even a pocket to keep your phone handy for those Instagram moments. And when you're wearing this thing, there are going to be plenty of Instagram moments.

1A and 1B. If you can figure out how to thread a needle, you can make this. Start by ripping the seams from the jeans to separate them in half.

2. Cut each half down the length of the leg to open it flat into one sheet of denim. Cut along the seam to halve the denim material again (not shown).

3. Fold over both sections of the pant-leg denim to make two strips of denim about as wide as a beverage can is tall. Use pins to hold the shape of the denim once it's the right shape, then sew the length of the pinned denim to make two long sashes. One sash will be the base for the bandolier, and the other will be the holsters for the cans.

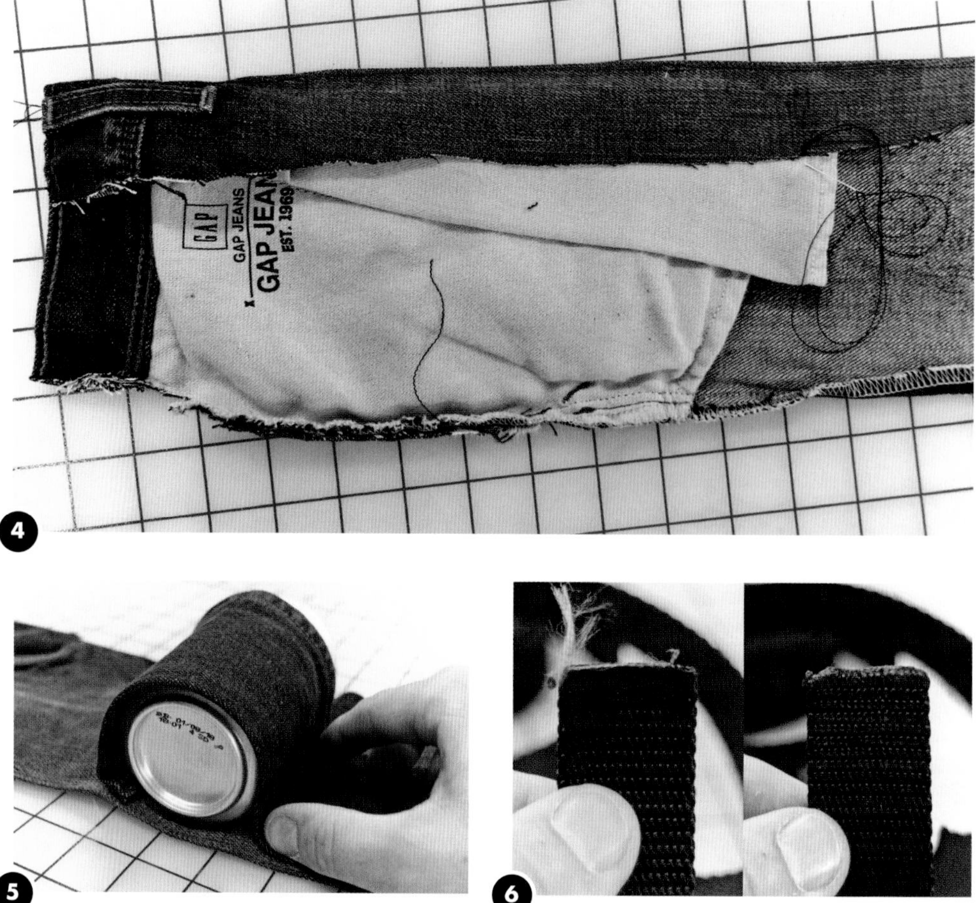

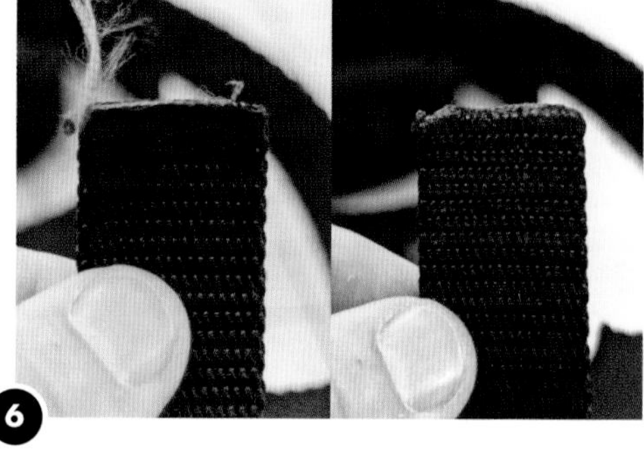

4. The sash with the former front pocket of the jeans is used as the base of the bandolier.

5. Sew one end of the holster sash to the base sash near the pocket, then place a beverage can under the holster sash and drape the sash over top. Hold the holster fabric over the can, against the backing sash, to determine where to sew the holster to the base and create a pocket for the can. Pin this location, remove the can, and sew the pocket with a single line of stitches. Continue these pockets along the length of the base sash until all pockets are created.

6. The pockets need bottoms to prevent the cans from falling out. An easy way to achieve this is by using nylon strapping available in fabric stores. When strapping is cut, it leaves a frayed edge, which can come unraveled over time. To prevent this, simply pass a lighter under the frayed edge to singe the plastic and melt the loose ends into a solid and clean edge. Cut strapping to span the length under the pockets, making sure to singe each cut end of the strapping.

7

7. Sew the strapping into place using a beverage can as a spacer. Repeat this for all can pockets on the bandolier.

8

8. Fold the end of the base sash to a taper and sew a length of strapping to the end. The clip end of the plastic buckle will attach here, so make sure to allow for plenty of extra strapping, which can be trimmed up later. Repeat this for the opposite end of the base sash, where the other half of the buckle will attach. Feed each half of the buckle through its respective end on the strapping. Wrap the sash around yourself to determine how much excess strapping you need. Then trim to length, singe the end to prevent fraying, and sew the strapping to prevent the buckle from coming off.

Now you're ready to be the beer commando at the next patio party, launching sudsy grenades to your friends for emergency hydration. At ease, soldier!

BOTTLE LOFT

MATERIALS AND TOOLS

- PAINT-STIRRING STICKS (OR SIMILAR THIN WOOD STRIPS)
- SMALL SAW
- NEODYMIUM MAGNETS
- DRILL AND SPADE BIT
- WHITE PAINT (OPTIONAL)
- UTILITY KNIFE
- TWO-PART EPOXY
- DOUBLE-SIDED MOUNTING TAPE
- SCISSORS FOR CUTTING TAPE

There's nothing quite like a refreshing cold one after a hard day of whatever, but sometimes it's hard to find room for food in your fridge alongside your beer supply. Take advantage of all that wasted vertical space between the shelves. How? By hanging bottles from the underside of a shelf, thus creating much-needed additional space below . . . for more bottles, of course.

1. Thin strips of wood will support the magnets that hold the bottles. You can use any thin strips of wood, but the frugal among us will use those paint-mixing sticks you can find free at most home improvement stores.

2. Place three bottles side by side in a straight line and then place a wood strip next to the bottles. Mark where the bases of the bottles fall on center and use a small saw to cut the thin wood to length.

3. Neodymium magnets are super strong and perfect for holding the weight of bottles by their metal caps. Find a spade bit of the same diameter as the magnets you are using.

4. If you use round magnets, you'll just need to drill holes partway through the wood strip; if you use square or rectangular magnets (like I did here), you'll need to trim the corners of your partially drilled holes with a utility knife to accommodate the square shape.

Sand the edges and corners smooth and rounded.

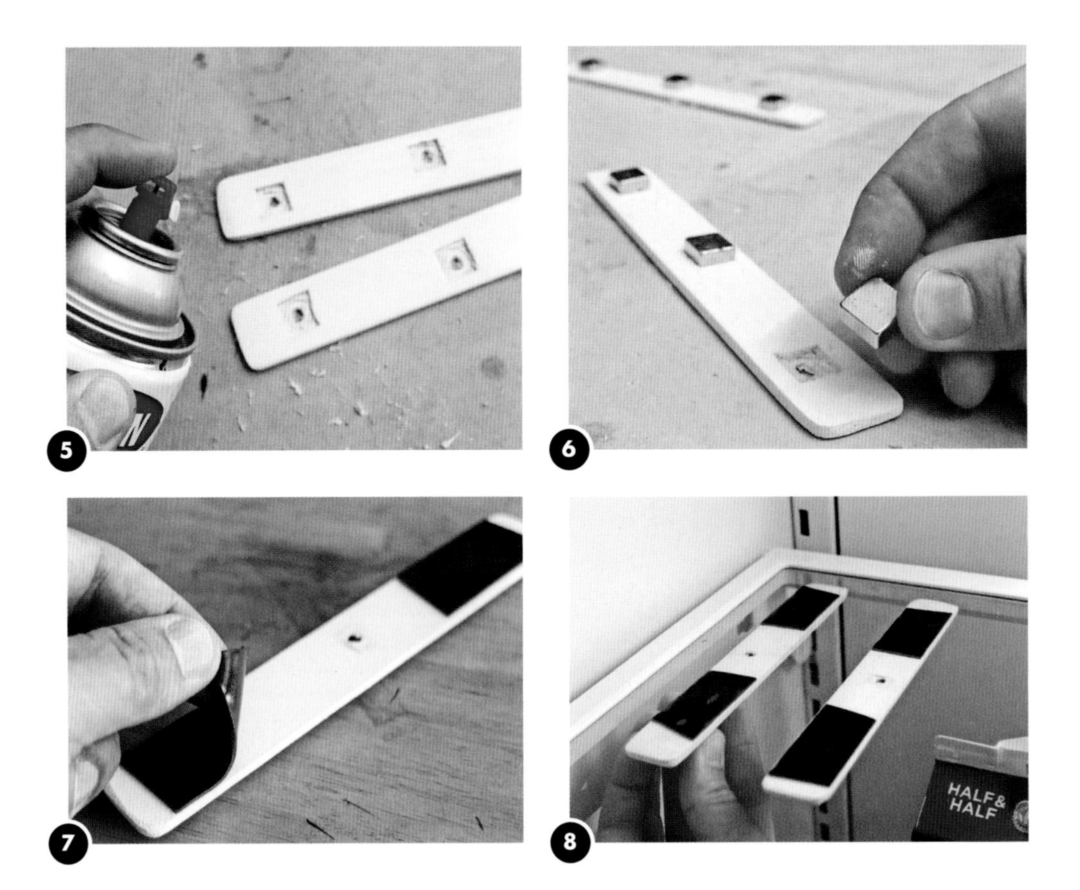

5. Most refrigerators are white inside. Painting the wood strips to match makes the bottle loft more visually appealing.

6. Strong epoxy will hold the magnets to the wood. Use a dab of epoxy in each drilled hole, then place one magnet into each and secure it in place until the epoxy has completely cured.

7. For the double-sided mounting tape to hold the bottle loft to the underside of the refrigerator shelf, you will need to remove the shelf from the fridge and allow it to acclimatize to room temperature—the tape will not stick to cold glass, plastic, or metal. While the fridge shelf warms up, cut small sections of the mounting tape and affix them to the back side of the bottle loft.

8. When the shelf is room temp, place it back in the fridge and stick the bottle loft to the underside of the shelf, ideally in the back corner to maximize fridge space. Press the bottle loft to the shelf to ensure it is securely adhered, then allow about an hour for adhesion before loading with bottles.

CAR CUISINE

MATERIALS AND TOOLS

- HEAVY-DUTY ALUMINUM FOIL
- BREAD
- CHEESE
- COLD CUTS (OPTIONAL)
- CAR WITH A MUFFLER
- STEEL WIRE
- STRONG STOMACH

There are times when the destination is more important than the journey. Like when you're driving through Kansas or New Mexico to get somewhere. Times like these are when stopping to enjoy a meal is not a high priority. Instead of trying to choke down some food at a terrible roadside diner, why not kill two birds with one stone: driving and cooking? It's easier than you think!

Though this trick can work for a variety of foods, the easiest thing to cook using this method is grilled cheese, partly because you can buy bread and cheese almost anywhere, but mostly because it's still safe to eat whether it's over- or undercooked.

1. Pull out a long sheet of thick aluminum foil and lay it down so the shiny side faces up. This will be the inside of our sandwich wrap. The dull side of the foil will absorb heat, which will force the sandwich to get hot, and the shiny side will reflect the heat inside the wrap. Construct your cheese sandwich however you like—adding cold cuts here is a good option. Wrap the sandwich tightly with foil.

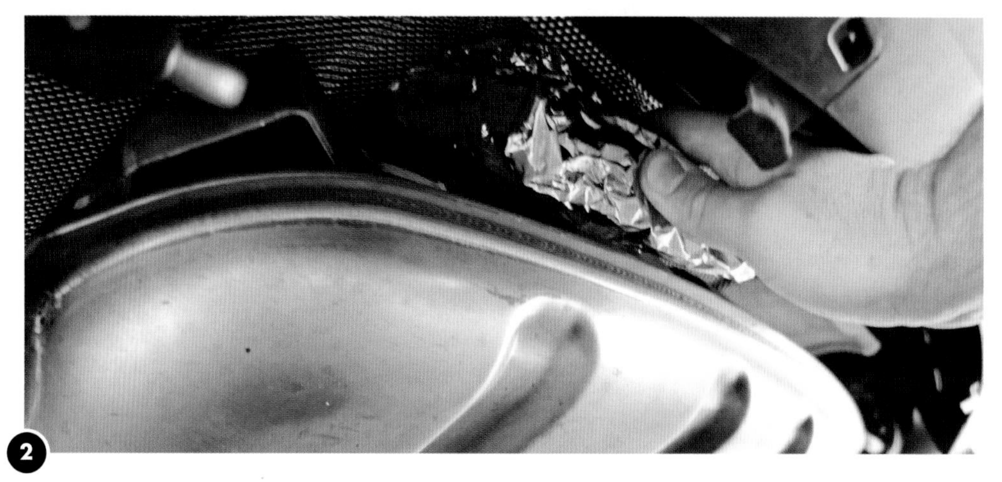

2. Looking under your car, find the muffler. In case you don't know, the muffler looks like a wide, squashed metal cylinder and has a tailpipe coming out of it. The muffler baffles the sound of exhaust gas leaving the engine so your car runs at sensible volumes. The exhaust gas is very hot and heats up the muffler. The muffler's temperature depends on what kind of engine and car you drive, as well as how you drive your car. However, under normal driving conditions (like on a road trip) a muffler can reach anywhere from 700 to 1,000°F (370 to 540°C). Above the muffler is a good place to wedge your sandwich to heat it up. Because mufflers are suspended from the car's undercarriage, they can move around a bit while you are driving. It's a good idea to secure your wrapped sandwich to the muffler with some steel wire. It's also a good idea to wait for the muffler to cool down a bit before sticking your hand up there.

Once your sandwich is secured to the muffler, drive on as normal. Check on your sandwich after about 30 minutes. By this time you should be able to notice how melty your cheese is and whether the sandwich needs more time on the "grill."

DISHWASHER LASAGNA

MATERIALS AND TOOLS

- FAVORITE LASAGNA RECIPE
- LARGE SINGLE-USE ALUMINUM BAKING PAN WITH LID
- ALUMINUM DUCT TAPE
- HOUSEHOLD DISHWASHER

Here's another deceptively simple idea: use your dishwasher to make dinner!

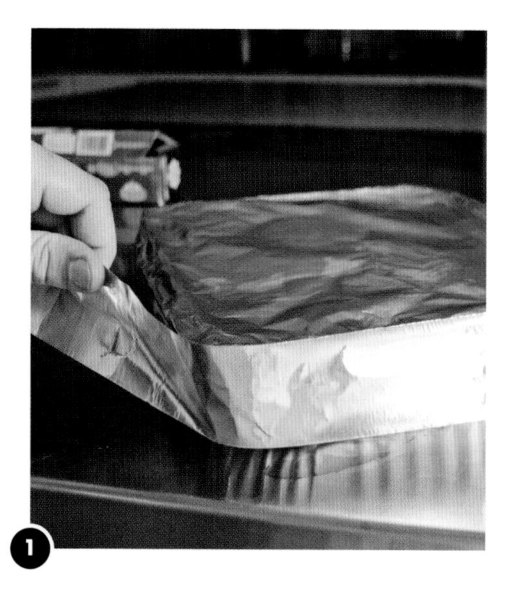

1. After gathering and prepping all the ingredients according to the recipe for your favorite lasagna (making sure any meat and vegetables are fully cooked), layer all the ingredients inside a single-use aluminum baking pan instead of a regular baking pan. Fill the pan almost full (making sure to use lots of cheese) and then cover it with the aluminum lid. Crimp the edges to create a seal, then use aluminum duct tape to make the seal watertight.

2. Load the sealed lasagna onto the top shelf of your dishwasher, along with all the rest of the dishes used to prepare the lasagna, and set the dishwasher to its hottest setting (without detergent). The hot water and steam will melt the cheese and finish the lasagna to perfection. After the cycle has finished, leave the dishwasher closed and allow the lasagna to rest inside for about 15 minutes before opening. Open dishwasher, remove lasagna, and serve!

JIGSAW MARTINI SHAKER

MATERIALS AND TOOLS

- **JIGSAW WITH BLADE**
- **STAINLESS-STEEL MARTINI SHAKER**
- **FOUR ZIP TIES**
- **WIRE SNIPS**

Break all the rules: enjoy an adult beverage while working with a power tools. Actually, it's not as dangerous as it sounds—as it turns out, the reciprocating motion of a jigsaw blade makes for a great martini mixer.

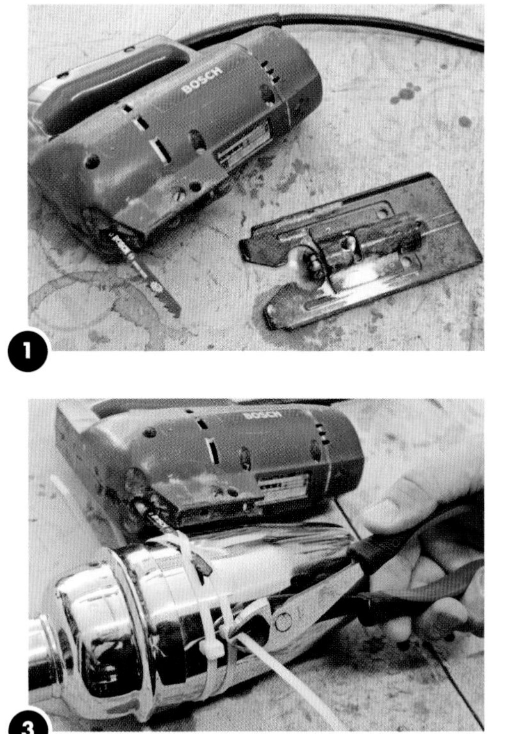

1. In order to maximize the full reciprocating travel of the jigsaw blade, you'll need to remove the tool's baseplate. Most jigsaws have a single large screw on the underside of the baseplate; removing this allows the entire baseplate to come off the unit.

2. Join two zip ties to create a longer zip tie. Do this twice to create two long zip ties, then wrap them around the martini shaker, crossing them at the blade as shown. A blade with longer teeth is helpful here for providing better grip on the zip ties. The zip ties should secure the shaker as near to the tip of the blade as possible, which will help ensure that the body of the saw does not interfere with the travel of the shaker. Attach the blade/shaker unit to the jigsaw to check that there is space for travel between the shaker and the body of the jigsaw.

3. Tighten all zip ties to remove any slack, then clip the tails of the ties to keep things tidy.

4. The mixer is functionally complete. Remove the blade/shaker unit from the jigsaw before filling with your cocktail ingredients. For me, it's 2 ounces of gin with ice.

5

6

5. Replace the top on the shaker and secure the blade/shaker back onto the jigsaw body. Holding the jigsaw vertically so the shaker is upright, engage the jigsaw trigger to begin shaking. The jigsaw does the manual work of shaking the cocktail in a way that no bartender can hope to match, mixing the beverage with flair and style.

6. With mixing complete, release the blade from the jigsaw and start pouring. The blade stays attached to the shaker, which makes pouring successive drinks easy. Empty the shaker, give it a quick rinse, and you're ready to mix the next cocktail.

-DUDE CRAFTS-
HIGH
FASHION

COIN RING

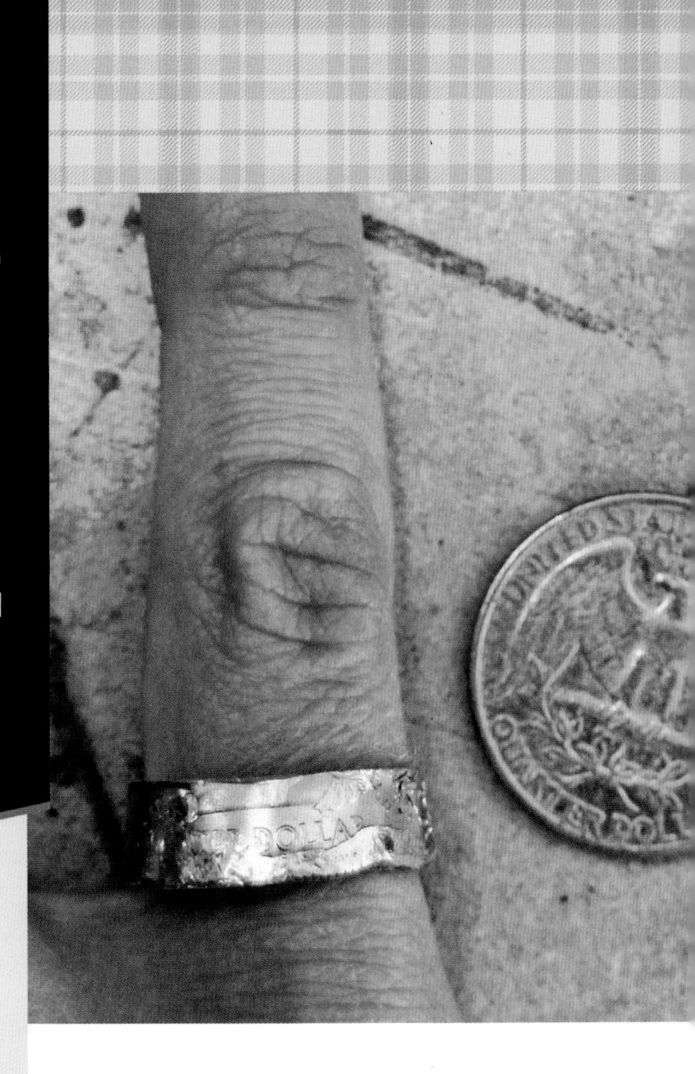

MATERIALS AND TOOLS

- US QUARTER OR SIMILARLY SIZED COIN
- DRILL AND STEPPED DRILL BIT, UP TO 1⅛-INCH DRILL BIT TO START OPENING
- NEEDLE-NOSE PLIERS
- MANDREL
- HAMMER
- EMERY CLOTH (220–1,000 GRIT)

Making a ring from a coin is an easy way to get started making jewelry, and the textured exterior of the resulting piece gives it a unique look that other rings don't have.

Despite what you've heard, defacing currency isn't illegal. What *is* illegal is defacing currency with the intent to use it as currency afterward. Since no sane person would think a reshaped coin is currency, this project is perfectly legal.

These rings are quick and easy to make, and they prove that manly jewelry can be achieved for as little as twenty-five cents, a little time, and a bit of elbow grease.

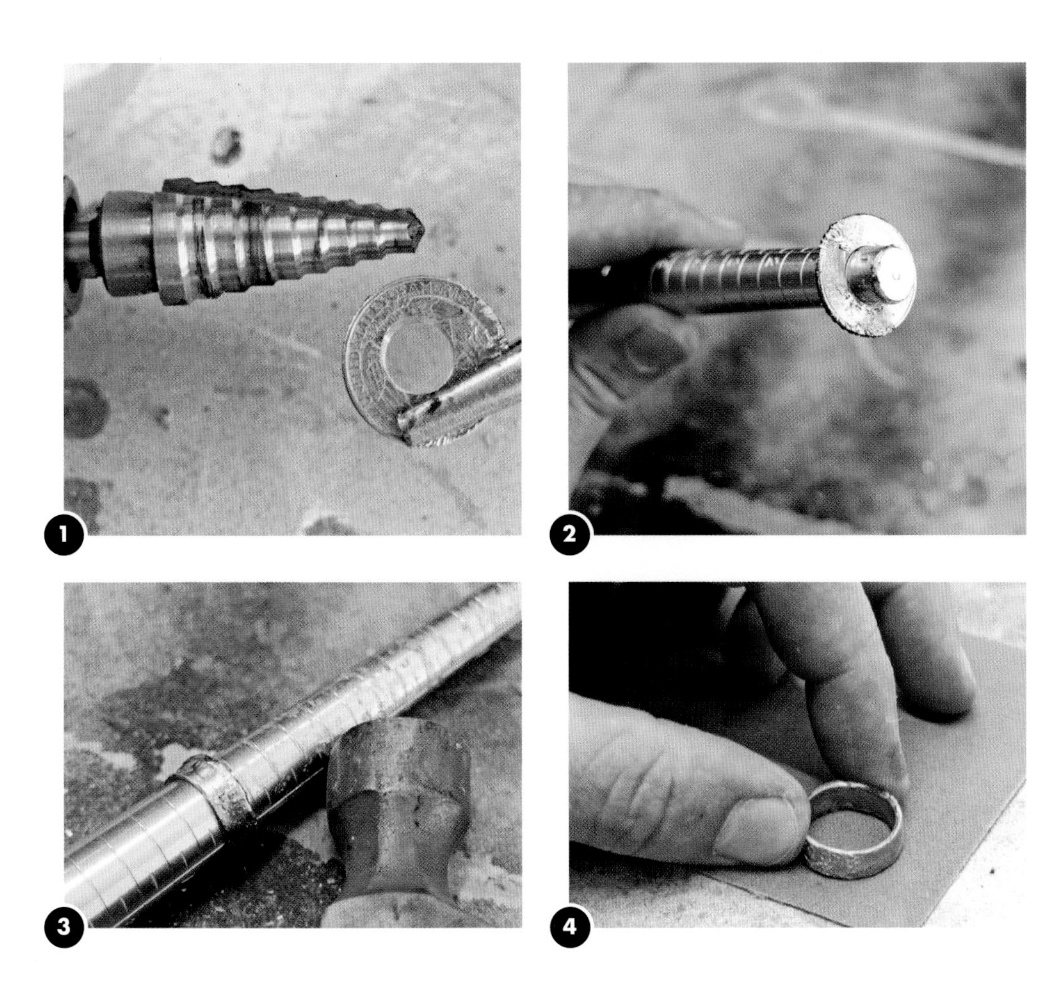

1. Quarters are a good choice for making a ring—they are large and thick with ample room to accommodate a finger. Start by drilling an opening in the middle of the coin while holding it firmly in a pair of needle-nose pliers. A stepped bit is a great tool for making the center opening because you have plenty of control over how large you make the opening, it's easier to make small adjustments in diameter, and the drilled edge is always chamfered (beveled) due to the incline between steps on the drill.

2. Bore out the center of the ring until the opening is wide enough to fit over the end of the mandrel.

3. Once you place the drilled-out coin over the tip of the mandrel, make light hammer blows on the coin. This will fold the outer edge of the coin downward and shape it over the mandrel. Continue hammering the coin to get it into a ring shape, while also hammering it up the tapered mandrel to the point where the ring is sized to fit your finger. Once the ring is the right shape and size, tap it back down to unseat it from the mandrel.

4. Smooth any rough edges with fine-grit emery cloth.

CUSTOM BLEACH-SPRAY T-SHIRT

MATERIALS AND TOOLS

- HOUSEHOLD BLEACH
- SPRAY BOTTLE
- COTTON-BLEND T-SHIRT
- CARDBOARD
- CARDSTOCK (AN OLD CEREAL BOX WORKS GREAT)
- PENCIL
- MARKER
- HOBBY KNIFE OR SCISSORS

There are plenty of great T-shirt designs out there, but sometimes you need something unique that you just won't find in a mall or big-box store—or on the back of everyone else in town. As it happens, making your own custom shirts is super simple, and there are loads of tweaks you can make to the process to achieve all sorts of one-off results. No two shirts will come out the same!

1. Start by pouring a 50/50 mixture of water and household bleach into a clean, empty spray bottle. When working with bleach, make sure you're in a well-ventilated area and wearing work clothes that you won't mind being slightly damaged if you accidentally spray or spill bleach on them.

2. Next, sketch out your design on cardstock; an empty cereal or cracker box cut open and turned inside out is perfect and plenty large for this. Sketch your design in pencil first to get the shapes right, then commit to the design in marker. The thicker lines will make the design easier to cut out. Use a hobby knife or scissors to make stencils by cutting out the shapes from the cardstock.

3. Place a large piece of cardboard inside your shirt—this will prevent the bleach solution from penetrating through and bleaching the back side of the shirt. Place it on your workbench with the side you want to make the design on facing up. Smooth out the shirt so there are no wrinkles. Taking the time to get the shirt perfectly flat here will pay off big time when it comes time to spray.

4

5

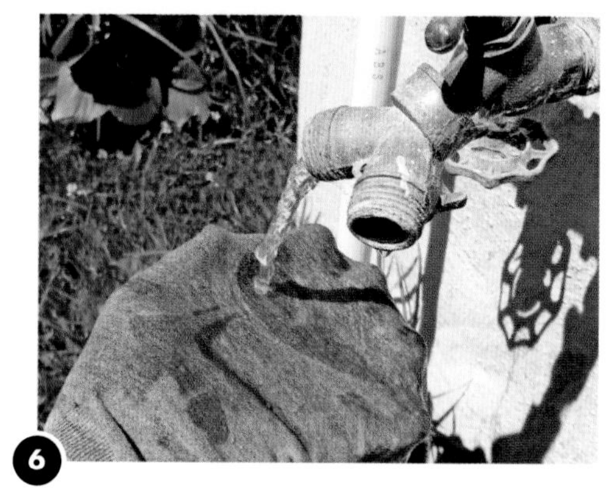

6

4. Arrange your stencils on the shirt, making sure they are flat against the fabric. If the stencils are bent and lift off the fabric, take a moment to gently bend them and lay them flat. When your stencils are flat and aligned you can begin spraying.

For best results, spray the bleach and water mixture from approximately 10 inches from the fabric, and from directly above. Applying a few gentle misting coats is more effective than a single heavy coat at closer range. A light misting over the entire stencil is all that's needed to achieve the effect.

5. Work quickly but carefully, as the thin cardstock will absorb the spray solution and begin to curl away from the fabric. After spraying, wait 30 to 60 seconds. The bleach will start to transform the shirt color around the stencils.

6. Once you have the contrast you want, remove the stencils. Massage the shirt under running water to ensure it's completely saturated and that all bleach is rinsed out. The first time you wash the shirt after wearing, make sure you do it separately from other laundry as there will still be some bleach in the fabric.

TIMING BELT

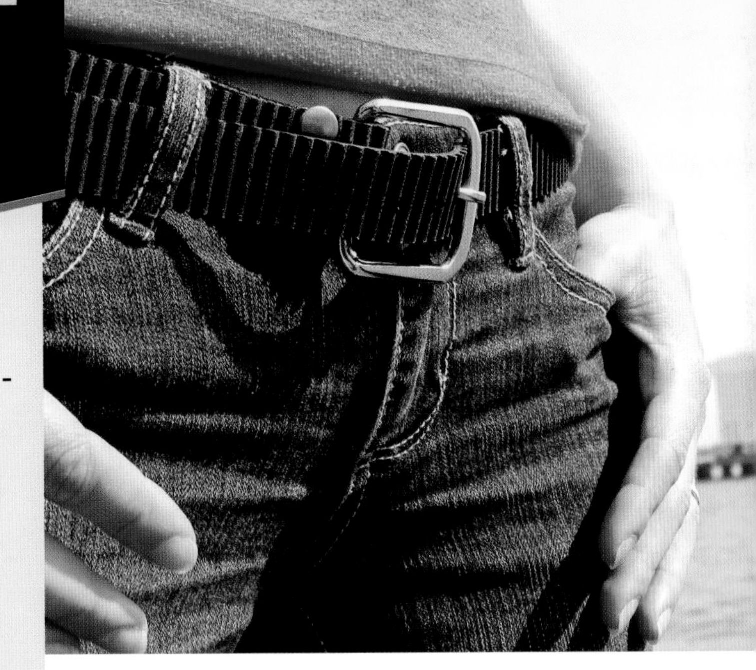

MATERIALS AND TOOLS

- BELT BUCKLE
- RIBBED AUTOMOTIVE TIMING BELT
- SCISSORS
- WIRE CLOTHING HANGER
- 100-GRIT SANDPAPER
- PROPANE TORCH
- CLOTHING SNAP RIVETS
- SMALL HAMMER
- HEAVY-DUTY SHEARING SCISSORS

More than just a cheeky play on words, this belt will keep your pants up and you fashionable. Whether you're a car guy or just someone who likes unusual things, this accessory will get your butt in gear.

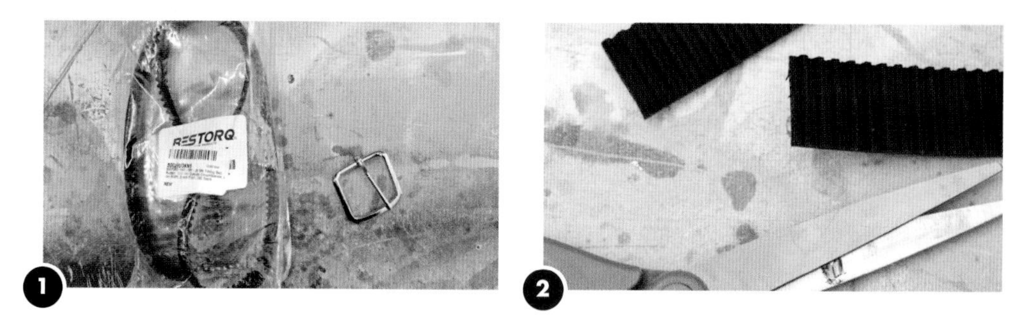

1. There are so many timing belts made to fit automobiles of all makes and manufacturers that it's not difficult to find one to fit your waistline. The belt seen here was about 32 inches in circumference.

2. Cut the belt between two of the ribs to break the loop.

3. Cut a 1½-inch slit lengthwise down the middle on one end of the belt, creating two thin tabs. These tabs will hold the buckle, but first we need to make clean holes in the belt though which to insert the snap rivets.

4. A piece of clothing hanger makes a good poking tool. Sand the end to a dull point, then use a propane torch to heat the tip of the hanger until red hot.

5. Push the hot poker through the ends of each of the two tabs to burn small openings for the snap rivets.

6A and 6B. Each side of the snap rivet comprises two parts that are hammered together to secure them in place.

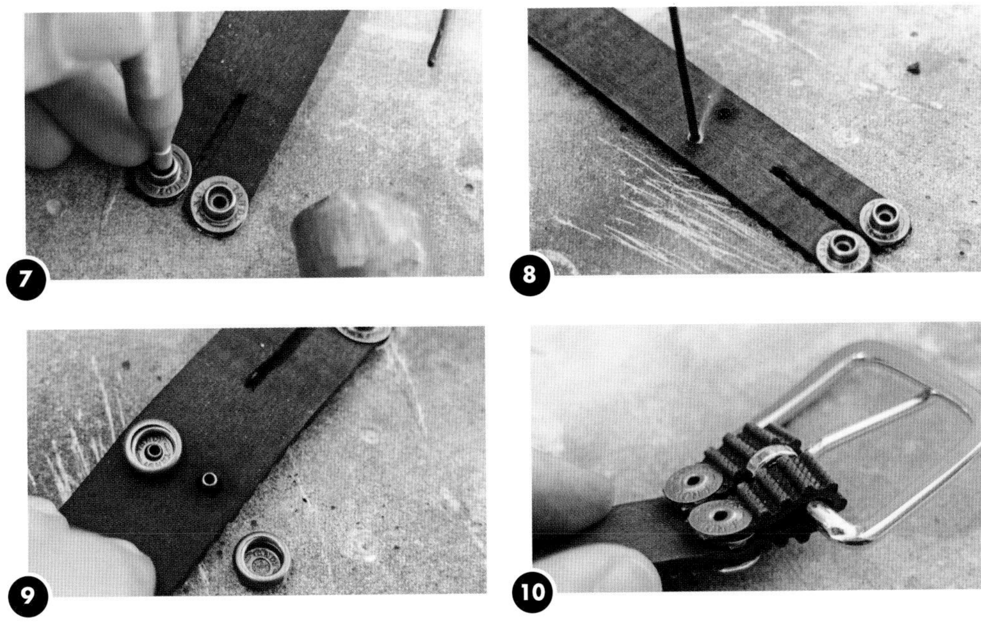

7. After both openings are poked in the small tabs of the belt, insert one half of each snap rivet in each hole and hammer them in to secure them to the belt.

8. Fold the tabs over the buckle to determine the best location for the mating rivets to be placed on the tabs. Once again, use the hot poker to make openings for the other halves of the snap rivets.

9. Hammer the remaining halves of the rivets in place.

10. The tabs fold over the frame of the buckle and are snapped closed with the rivets to secure the buckle, while the buckle's prong fits in the opening between the tabs.

11. Use your same old heated poker to make a hole every inch or so for the buckle prong.

12. To clean things up, cut the belt's sharp corners at 45-degree angles.

-DUDE CRAFTS-

THE GREAT OUTDOORS

BOOZE-BOTTLE ICE SHEATH

MATERIALS AND TOOLS

- EMPTY 2-LITER PLASTIC BOTTLE
- HOBBY KNIFE
- GLASS BOTTLE OF YOUR FAVORITE BOOZE (AT LEAST 40 PERCENT ABV)

Bring a touch of class to your next outdoor party by serving your hooch in a sheath of pure ice! Friends will be wowed, women will swoon—and you will be the coolest host ever!

1. Making your own booze-bottle ice sheath is incredibly easy. Find any empty 2-liter plastic soda bottle and use a hobby knife to remove the top of the bottle at the shoulder where the neck tapers. Wash out the inside of the bottle.

2. Center your full bottle of booze in the opened 2-liter soda bottle, then fill the plastic bottle about three-quarters of the way up with water. Do *not* fill entirely with water—remember science class? Water expands when it freezes, and if the soda bottle is full, you will end up with a mess in your freezer.

3. To keep the booze bottle centered in the plastic bottle, wrap some wadded-up paper towels around the top of the glass bottle at the lip of the plastic bottle.

4. Place this water-filled assembly upright in the freezer overnight. Once it's frozen, remove it from the freezer, run the plastic soda bottle under cold water, and gently pull the glass bottle with its new ice sheath from the plastic.

5. To make pouring easier, I usually wrap the ice with a bar rag to keep my fingers from freezing. Now when you make a drink for a guest, they will always have the coldest beverage you can offer. Cheers!

THE GENTLEMAN'S GOLF CLUB (OR SKI POLE)

MATERIALS AND TOOLS

- GOLF CLUB
- FOOD-SAFE VINYL TUBING (1/4-INCH O.D.)
- PROPANE TORCH OR HEAT GUN
- PLIERS
- DRILL AND BIT
- PLASTIC MINI LIQUOR BOTTLE

It's widely acknowledged that stopping off at the nineteenth hole often entails a few adult beverages. But how to survive out there on the links in the meantime, with the hot sun beating down? Now, bringing a few shots of your favorite liquor onto the course is easy thanks to the drinking reservoir hidden inside the Gentleman's Golf Club—it's just what the pro shop ordered. (Actually, they didn't order it, so let's learn how to make one.)

This same concept can also be applied to ski poles.

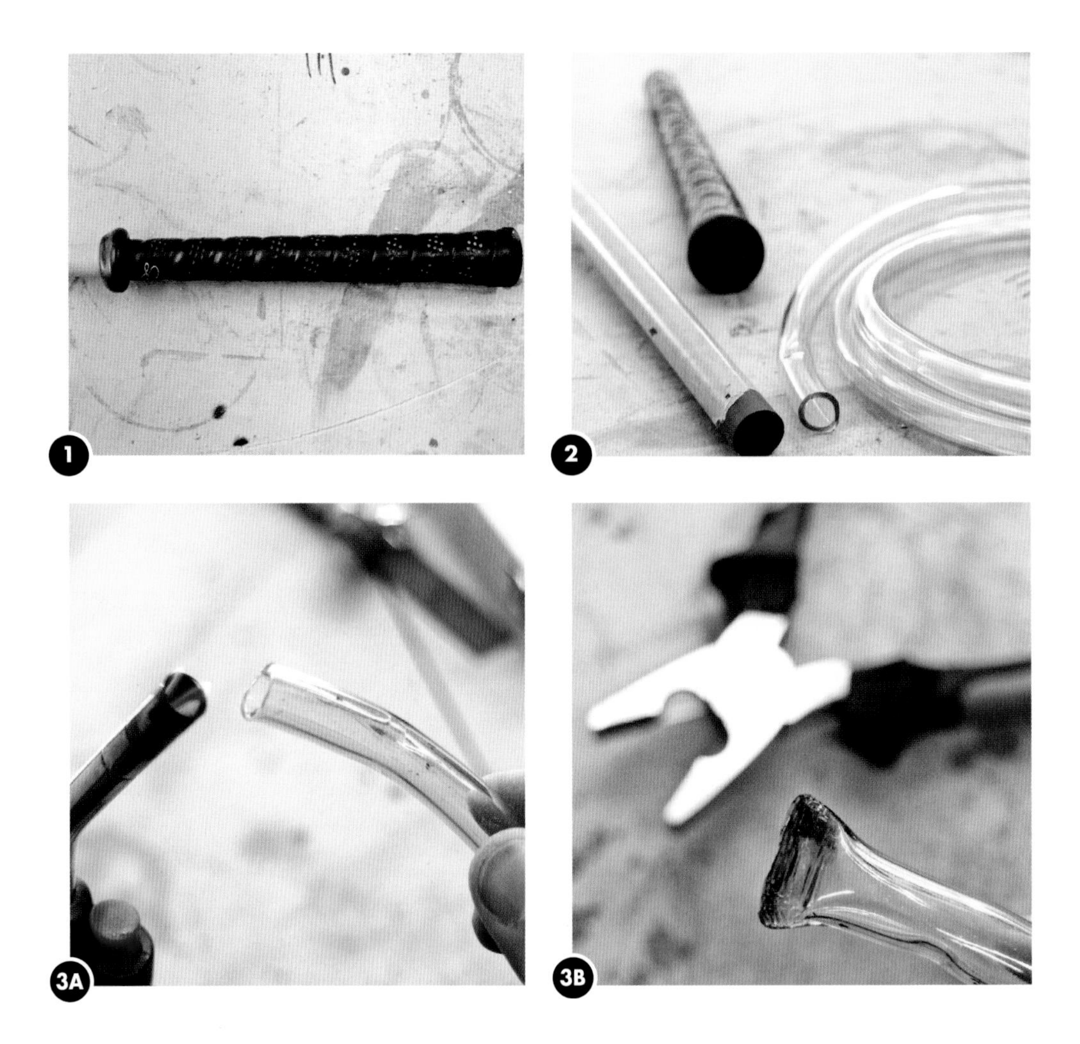

1. Start by rolling up the rubber grip of the club handle to remove it and expose the hollow shaft where your drink reservoir will be placed.

2. You will be making the drink reservoir from food-safe vinyl tubing, which you can typically find in hardware and homebrew stores.

3A and 3B. The tubing needs to be closed at one end using a propane torch or heat gun. Heat the end of the tube near (but not directly in) the flame, if using a torch. Use pliers to fuse the end closed. When it's cool, test the fused end to make sure it has no leaks. Feed the fused end of the vinyl tube into the hollow club shaft to determine the length of vinyl tubing needed. With the tubing inserted into the club, cut it to length so the cut end is slightly higher than the top of the shaft.

4. Cut off the threaded top of the plastic mini liquor bottle including the cap.

5. The bottle top is friction-fitted to the vinyl tube and becomes the screw cap for the hidden reservoir.

6. Drill an opening into the top of the rubber handle, then push the threaded liquor cap onto the top of the vinyl tube. The tube inserts inside the threaded bottle neck and should be held in place by friction, though you can use a small amount of glue at the base of the threads to hold the tubing in place.

7. With the reservoir inside the shaft, unroll the rubber handle back onto the shaft to complete the gentleman's golf club. All that's left is to fill the reservoir with your liquor of choice. If you don't score a hole-in-one, at least you can still have a good day!

PARACORD **BULLWHIP**

MATERIALS AND TOOLS

- **PARACORD (500 TO 600 FEET IN MULTIPLE COLORS)**
- **BBs OR SHOT**
- **SCISSORS**
- **ELECTRICAL TAPE (TWO TO THREE ROLLS)**
- **LIGHTER OR CANDLE**
- **STEEL ROD FOR HANDLE**
- **NAIL**
- **THIN STRIP OF LEATHER (OPTIONAL)**

Few things are more satisfying than the crack of a whip. But cracking a whip that you made yourself may be one of them. Making your own paracord whip is surprisingly easy but requires a bit of patience for weaving the strands together.

1. To make the weighted core of the paracord whip, take three 6-foot lengths of paracord and pull back the covering to reveal the strands of string inside. You will need to pull out the strings to make room for the BBs to go inside.

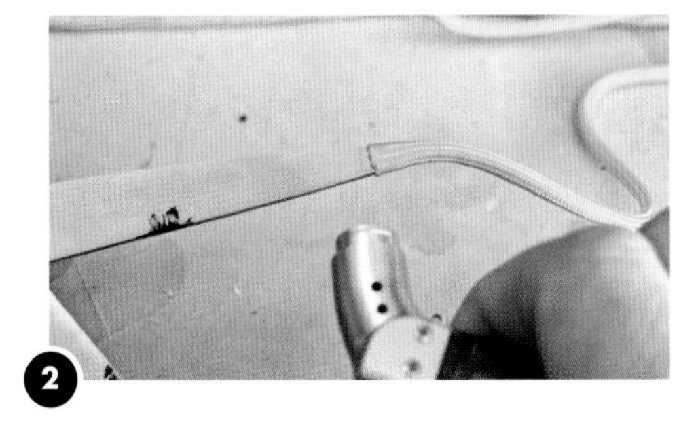

2. When the insides of the paracord sections have been removed, place the open end of one paracord section on the pointy end of open scissors and quickly run a lighter over the end to melt the frayed covering and widen the opening. Repeat this process for each end of the three sections of gutted paracord. Set aside the strand guts for later.

3. The BBs should easily slide into the widened opening of the paracord.

4. The BBs can be squeezed down the length of the paracord by using the rounded side of a tool against a flat workbench. Repeat this process for all three gutted paracord sections until they are almost packed with BBs, leaving about 1 foot without, which will be attached to the handle.

5. Group the three sections of BB-filled paracord lengthwise and use electrical tape to bind them together, leaving the handle section of the paracord unwrapped.

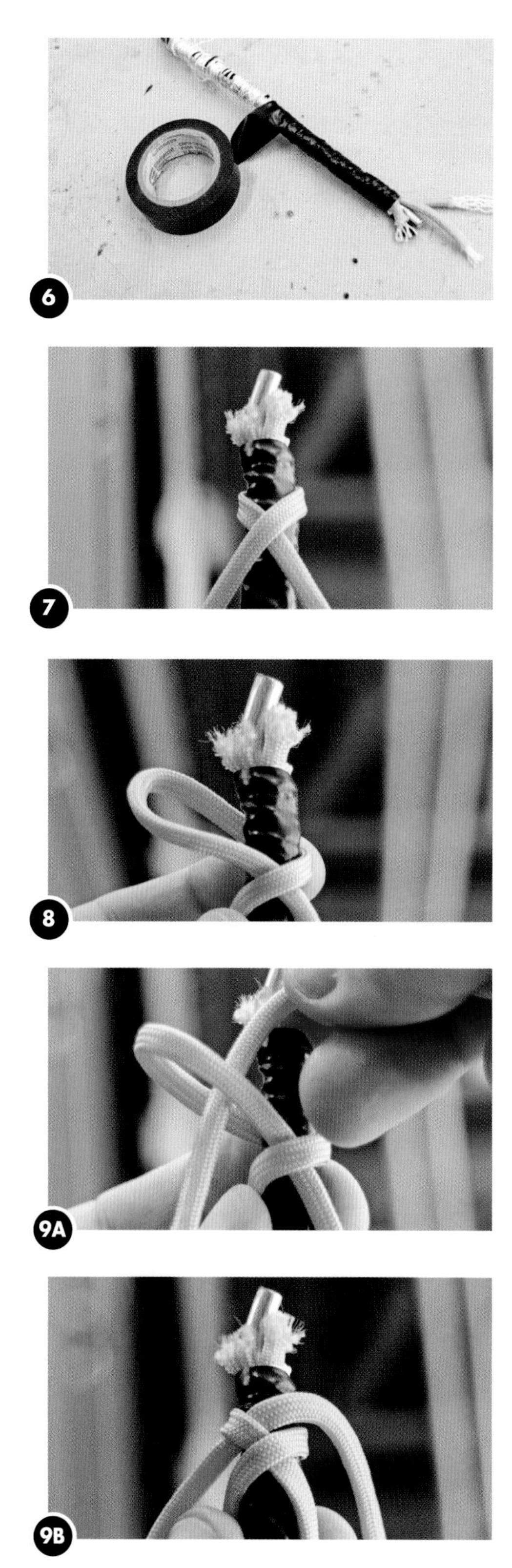

6. Take another three sections of 6-foot paracord lengths and group them together with the bound BB paracord, ensuring the new grouping is even around the circumference. Bind together with more electrical tape, making a bundle of six paracord sections. Place the steel rod in the middle of the bundle and hold it in place with the guts from a stripped paracord, then secure the handle with more electrical tape. This is the core of the paracord whip.

Plait 1

To build up the layers around the core, successive wrappings are braided on top of each other; these are called plaits. Secure the core to a sturdy work surface so the handle is facing upwards.

Paracord cuts

Two 10-foot lengths of paracord

7. Find the midpoint of one section of 10-foot paracord and drape it on the back of the handle, pulling the paracord toward you and crossing it.

8. Pull the bottom section of paracord up to make a small opening.

9A and 9B. Feed the second 10-foot section through the opening to halfway and pull the opening closed.

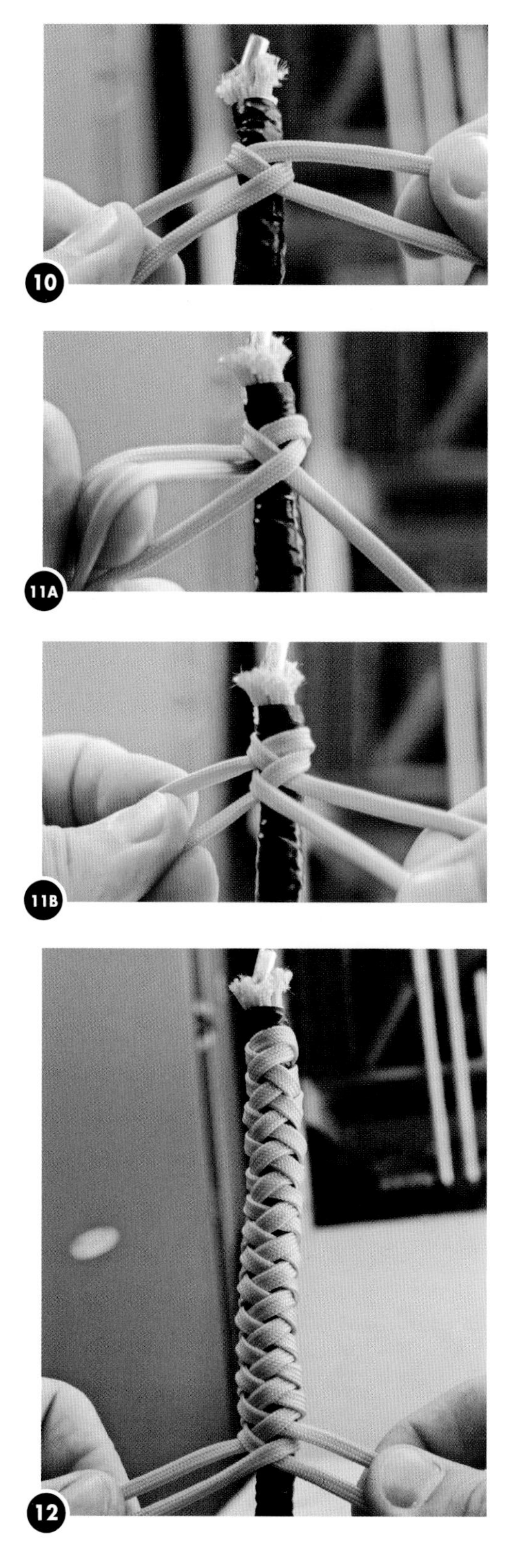

10. Gently pull the paracord leads away from the handle. You should see the lengths of paracord stacked on top of each other vertically; these are the four lengths of paracord that will be plaited together.

11A and 11B. To start plaiting, take the strand that's highest in the stack and bring it around the back of the handle to the front and over the lowest strand in the stack. This sounds more complicated than it really is—follow along with the pictures and you'll have made the first plait. This simple arrangement of paracord is how the entire whip will be made.

Gently pull the paracord sections away from the handle and again find the strand highest in the stack.

Repeat the process of passing it around the back of the handle to the front and then over the lowest strand.

12. Continue this down the entire length of the whip core until you run out of paracord.

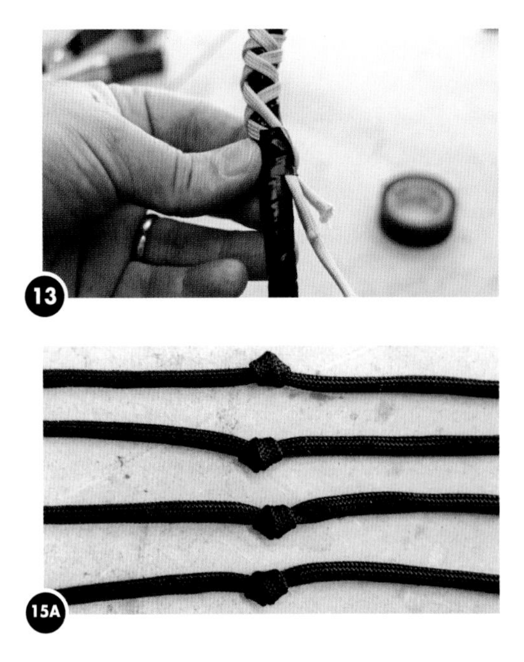

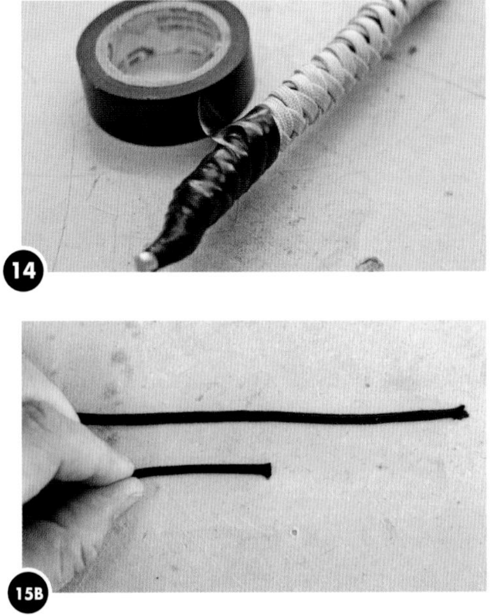

13. When you reach the end of the 10-foot sections of paracord, wrap the ends with electrical tape to prevent the plait from unraveling.

14. Wrap the entire plait with electrical tape.

PLAIT 2

Paracord cuts

Two 14-foot lengths
One 10-foot length
One 6-foot length

15A and 15B. Find the midpoint of the 14-foot sections and tie a knot. For the other two paracord sections, tie a knot 4 inches to one side of the midpoint.

16A and 16B. This second plait is just like the first one but uses two strands to start instead of one. Drape the 14-foot long sections of paracord around the back of the handle and cross them around the front.

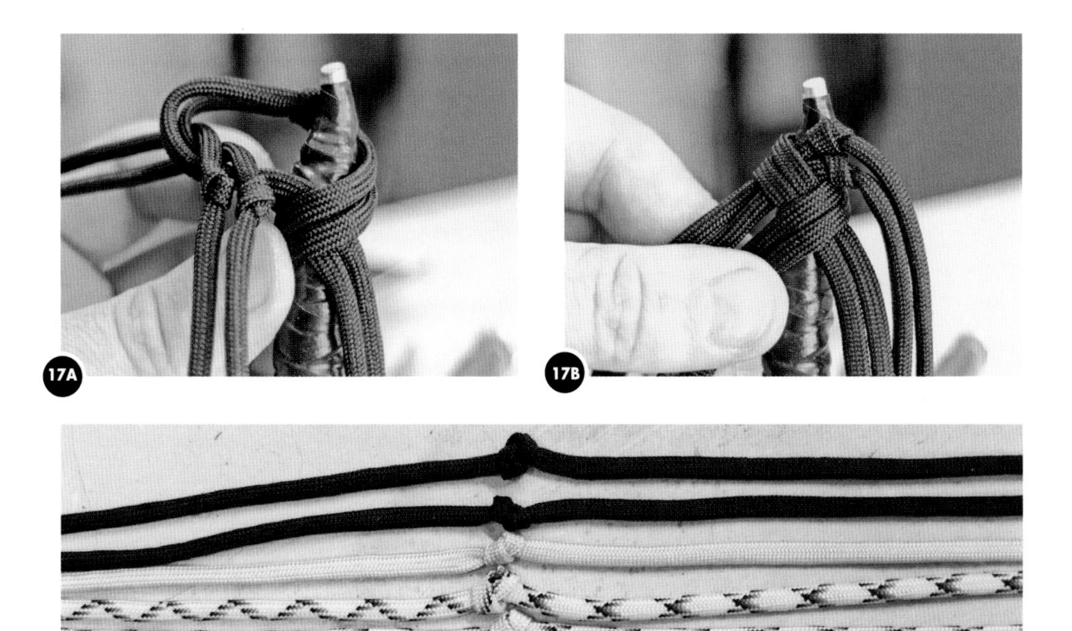

17A and 17B. As with the first plait, pull up one side of both strands to create an opening and then feed through the 10- and 6-foot sections of paracord. Pull the 14-foot sections tight to lock in the new strands.

Just like before, take the highest strand and bring it around the back of the handle to the front and then over the lowest two strands. Keep plaiting down the length of the whip. When the shortest length of paracord nears the end, lay the end along the length of the whip and continue plaiting over the end, now plaiting with one less strand. The reason the shorter sections of paracord were offset 4 inches is so they would end at different lengths along the whip and taper out.

When all paracord sections have been used, wrap the end and the entire length again with electrical tape.

PLAIT 3

Paracord cuts

Two 20-foot lengths
One 19-foot length
One 14-foot length
One 8-foot length
One 5-foot length

18. Find the midpoint of all the lengths of paracord and tie knots offset from the midpoints by 4 inches, as with plait #2. Since this is the plait that will show on your whip, choose your paracord colors and arrangement carefully.

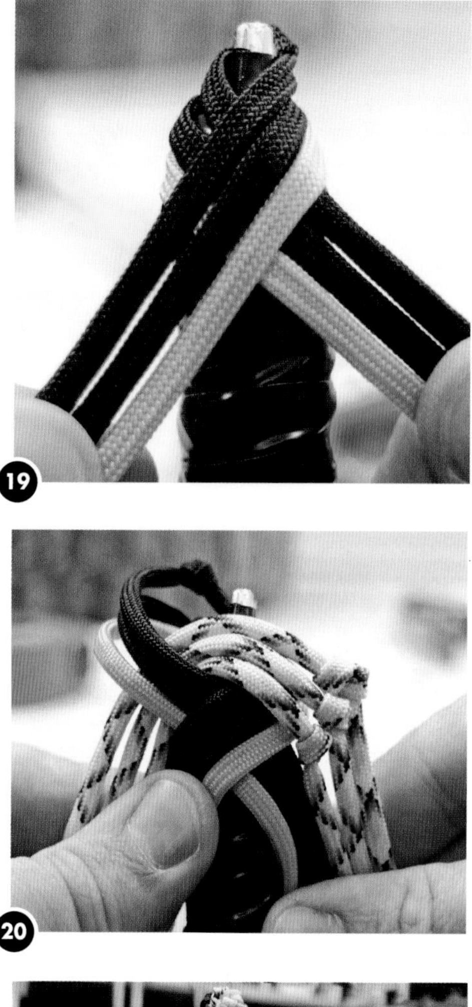

19. Drape the 20- and 19-foot lengths of paracord around the back of the handle at the knot, bring to the front, and cross over.

20. As before, push the lower lengths upward to make an opening and feed the remaining paracord lengths through to the knot.

21. Gently pull the loop closed. Same as before, plait starting with the highest strand on the stack bringing the strand around the back of the handle to the front. For this plait we'll go under the first two strands, over the middle two, and then under the lowest two strands.

Continue plaiting down the length of the whip. When a section of paracord is close to ending, lay it flat along the whip and continue to plait over it. When you reach the end of the whip, stop plaiting and tie off the strands of paracord to keep the plait secure.

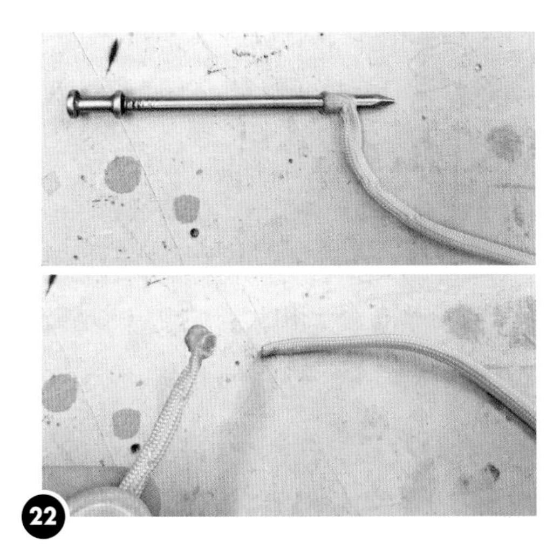
22

23

CRACKER

22. The whip is mostly done, but to really make it official, it needs a whip cracker. Cut a 2-foot length of paracord and remove any strands inside. Insert a nail into one end of the paracord length and use a lighter to melt the end to prevent fraying. Push the nail through the wall of the paracord about ½ inch from the end and ream it to about the same diameter as the paracord thickness, then use the lighter at this new opening to seal the shape.

23. Remove the nail and feed the opposite end of the 2-foot paracord length through to create a loop. Shorten the loop and tie the 2-foot paracord section to the top of the whip.

Take some of the paracord guts, or a piece of thin leather, and tie it to the loop opening at the top of the whip. Close the loop tightly to secure the cracker in place.

Your paracord whip is now complete—but a whip is no good unless you know how to crack it. Improperly cracking a whip is a good way to smack yourself in the face. In case it's not obvious, make sure you're in an open area before cracking your whip, away from any people or obstructions. Do not crack whip at or near people or animals, they will be very upset with you.

The cattleman's crack is the easiest method, and while it does take a little practice to get right, the technique is simple.

First, stand straight with the whip in one hand. In one motion, lift your arm up and back. While the whip is traveling backward, bring your arm forward in a sharp motion. The crack will happen behind your head. The trick to perfecting the cattleman's crack is to keep your arm and whip in line and as straight vertically as possible.

Once you've done one successful crack, successive ones will come easier. The same holds true for making a paracord whip—the first one may seem challenging, but the next one will be much easier.

POLAR-BEAR TUBES

MATERIALS AND TOOLS

- PVC PIPE (ANY DIAMETER, CUT TO FIT INTERIOR LENGTH OF COOLER)
- PVC ENDCAPS (TO FIT PIPE DIAMETER)
- SAW
- PVC CEMENT
- PERMANENT MARKER

When packing a cooler for a day at the lake or park, regular ice packs just aren't going to cut it. Keep things extra cold with ice tubes made to fit the length of your cooler. Custom-sized cooling tubes give you maximum cooling surface area to keep your contents cold longer.

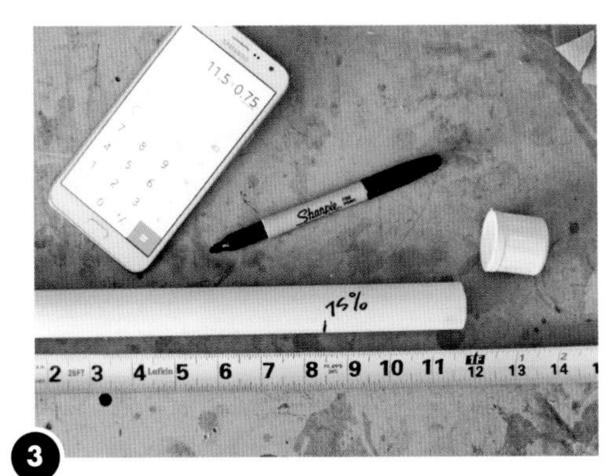

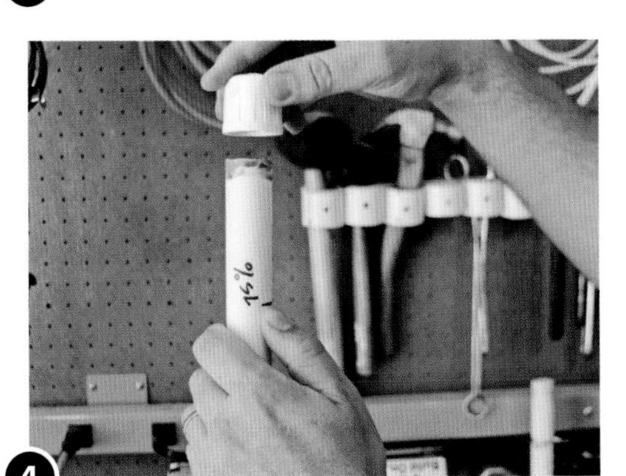

1. Measure the interior length of the cooler you want to keep cold, then use a saw to cut a PVC tube about 1 inch shorter than your measurement. This allowance will account for the endcaps to be added to the tube. When it comes to choosing a pipe diameter, a wider tube will give you more cooling surface area but also take up more space inside your cooler.

2. Close one end of the PVC tube with an endcap and PVC cement. This cement dissolves plastic; when two pieces are placed together, the melting creates a permanent weld within seconds.

3. We're almost ready to fill the tube with water. Because water expands as it freezes, the tube cannot be filled entirely or it will crack as the ice expands. Instead, you'll want to fill about 75 percent of the tube with water, so measure the tube length and multiply the measurement by 0.75. Mark the length on the tube, measuring from the sealed end and fill the tube to the marked level.

4. After ensuring the outside of the tube is dry, cement the remaining endcap on the open end to seal the water inside. Now toss these tubes into the freezer to turn them into ice torpedoes.

SWEDISH TORCH

MATERIALS AND TOOLS

- LOG
- CHAINSAW OR LARGE HANDSAW

Known by a few different names, the Swedish Torch is a very old method of making a long-lasting fire from a single log. The fire requires minimal harvesting of materials, and the flat top of the log doubles as a cooking surface. But don't spend money on a premade one at a home center—making your own Swedish torch is incredibly easy and a unique way to make your next camping trip more memorable. Take into account, however, that some states may place restrictions on wood that can be brought in to state-run campgrounds.

You can easily obtain large log sections from your local arborist, the roadside, or (as I have recently discovered) your local golf course after its semiannual pruning sessions. Wood that has been allowed to dry for a season or more is best. I used a chainsaw to make quick work of this project, but a large handsaw will also work if you have a bit of patience.

1. Chainsaws are handy tools that make quick work of cutting wood but can be dangerous if used incorrectly. The chainsaw blade cuts along the bar with the chain moving away from you from the top and back toward you on the bottom. Always cut using the bottom of the bar with the wood up against the engine body. *Never cut with the top of the bar!* There are fixed teeth where the chain disappears into the engine body that hold the wood in place while the chain blade makes the cut. Never force the chainsaw through the wood, let the chain cut the wood slowly and in a controlled manner.

2. Start by placing your log upright on a flat and sturdy area. Make a cut straight down, partially bisecting the log. Stop about halfway down the log's height. Move around the stump and make another cut perpendicular to the first, again stopping halfway down the length of the log. Create two more cuts in between the first two, all stopping around halfway.

3. You should end up with a shape on top resembling an eight-piece pie. That's it—you're done! I swept up the sawdust and saved it for an ignition aid in the Swedish torch.

4. Place the Swedish torch into your fire pit with the pie segments facing upward. Load up the troughs between the cuts with a little kindling and some of the sawdust, then ignite to start the torch. The burn will be slow at first but will escalate quickly as the thin pie segments catch fire. From start to finish I've had torches last about two hours, with the first hour or more perfect for cooking.

Though the Swedish torch method is certainly more work up front than buying firewood from the camp host, there's no other method that provides both fire and a flat cooking top—and the Swedish torch is also much less work once it's burning.

-DUDE CRAFTS-
CUTTING-
EDGE
DESIGN

AUTOMATIC SHOWERHEAD SOAPER

MATERIALS AND TOOLS

- NEW HOSE-END LAWN FEEDER
- HOSE-TO-SHOWER THREADED ADAPTER
- HAND-HELD SHOWER-ARM MOUNT
- TEFLON PLUMBING TAPE
- EMPTY LEMON- OR LIME-JUICE CONCENTRATE BOTTLE

Who has the time (or the will) to bother lathering in the shower when hungover? Why not take lazy showers to a whole new level by adding a soap sudser to your showerhead? This bathroom project is equal parts efficiency and sloth, and it will keep you clean even when you don't feel like it.

1

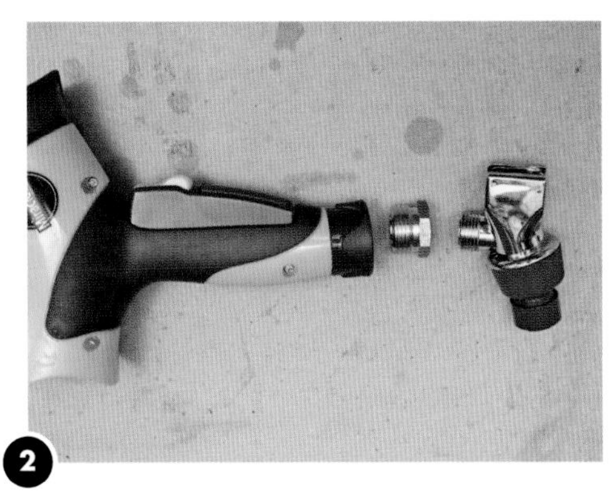

2

3

1. A lawn feeder is basically a bottle with a hose attachment. Water from the hose feeds through the bottle on its way out, mixing with whatever fertilizer products are placed in the bottle to feed the lawn. Instead of fertilizer, however, we're going to use body wash.

2. You can use a brass fitting (center) to connect the feeder's hose attachment to the smaller threads of a shower head. A showerhead holder (right) will give the feeder attachment the range of motion it needs by allowing you to bend the feeder upward into a more normal showerhead angle.

3. Use Teflon tape on all metal threads.

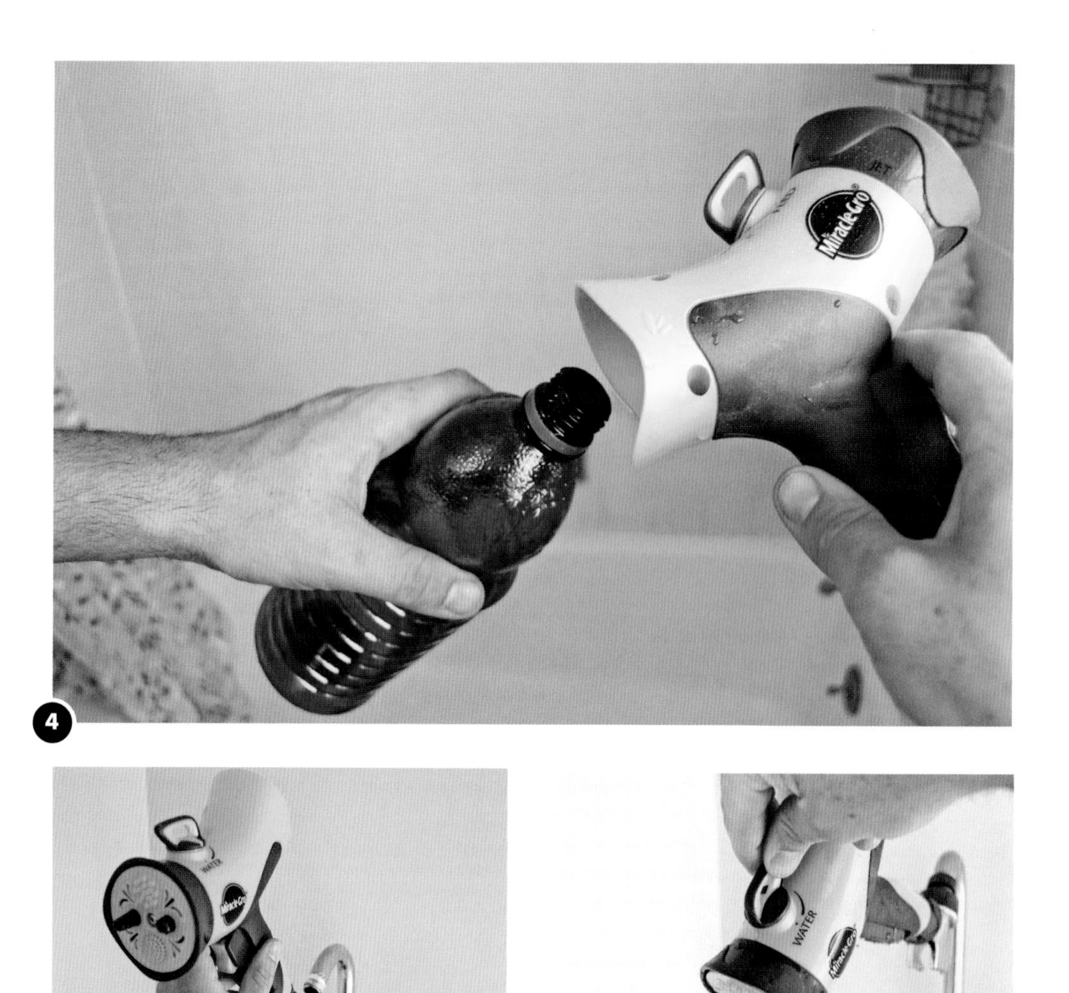

4. A regular shower-gel bottle won't fit the feeder's threads. However, it turns out that bottles used for lemon and lime juices are narrow enough to fit into the feeder's bottle cavity, and their threads will secure to the feeder unit. Perfect!

5. Now just unscrew the boring old conventional showerhead and attach the new soaper unit you've assembled.

Fill the juice container with your favorite shower gel and then screw the inverted bottle into the feeder unit.

6. The knob on the top of the unit shown here allows the user to control the amount of shower gel used. When the knob is closed, the shower shoots water only. There's nothing like being clean and lazy all at the same time!

BARBIE BOTTLE OPENER

MATERIALS AND TOOLS

- DOLL OR ACTION FIGURE
- BOTTLE OPENER
- E6000 ADHESIVE
- 10MM-DIAMETER NEODYMIUM MAGNETS
- ROTARY TOOL WITH CUTTING WHEEL

Terrify your kids and delight your friends! Give Barbie or Ken or GI Joe a more exciting duty than entertaining the young ones—namely, opening your favorite bottles. A 1:9 scale doll (approximately 8 inches tall) is ideal for this project, in which the doll is modified to split open at the torso and reveal a bottle opener. Perfect for clandestine capped beverages.

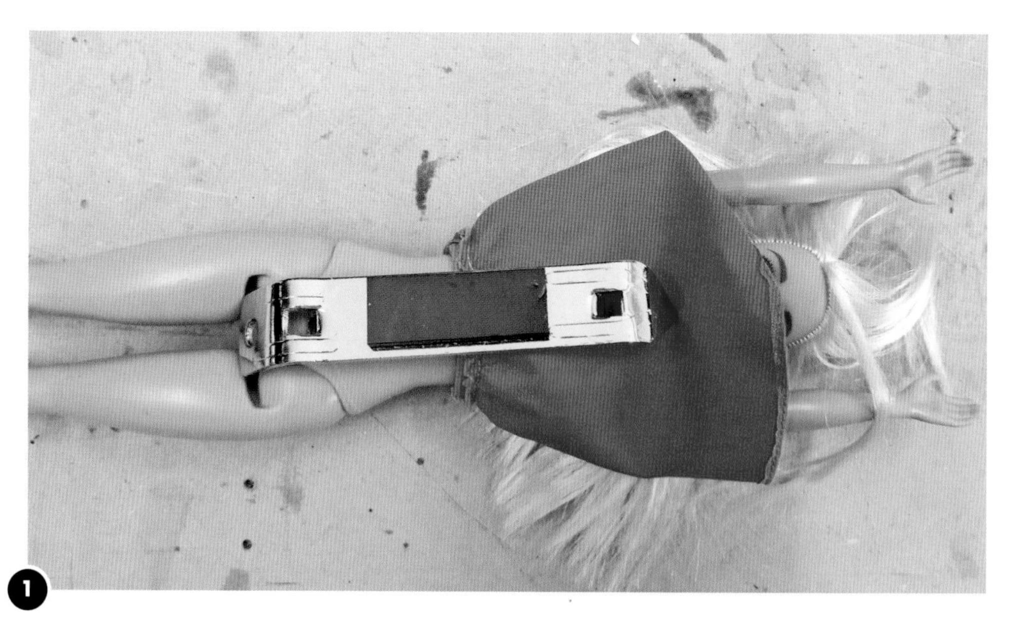

1. To start, align your opener with your doll to find the best placement.

2. Next, use your rotary tool with a cutting wheel to bisect your doll at the belly button. Clean up any burrs from the cut and test-fit the bottle opener inside the doll's upper cavity. Note how much the opener sticks out from the torso—you'll need some of the end exposed to open bottles, of course, but not enough to prevent the bottom of the doll from being placed back onto the torso.

3. Since you only need the bottle-cap end of the opener, if necessary you can cut off the pointed puncturing end using a rotary tool with cutting wheel to make the length work for the doll being used.

4. I use my favorite adhesive, E6000, to glue the opener into the upper part of the doll. E6000 is a semiflexible glue with crazy adhesive properties. Once it's set, there's no going back. Glue the opener into the upper part of the doll and leave it to set completely, which will take about 24 hours.

5. Small neodymium magnets on each half of the doll will rejoin the two halves when the opener's not in use. Start by gluing two magnets into the top portion with more E6000 and allowing the glue to cure completely. Then reference the locations of the magnets on the top half and use glue to secure the bottom-half magnets so that they line up.

6. Once all the glue is completely dry, the two halves can be placed together, hiding the doll's secret utility. If you're using a doll like this one, the dress will hide the split in the torso. All that's left now is for Barbie to crack open a few cold ones!

SUCTION-CUP SHOWER HOLDERS

MATERIALS AND TOOLS

- **SMALL SUCTION CUPS**
- **ELASTIC HAIR TIES**

When you've run out of shelf space in your shower and there's no room to store more bottles, these simple shower holders might be the answer to your clutter conundrum.

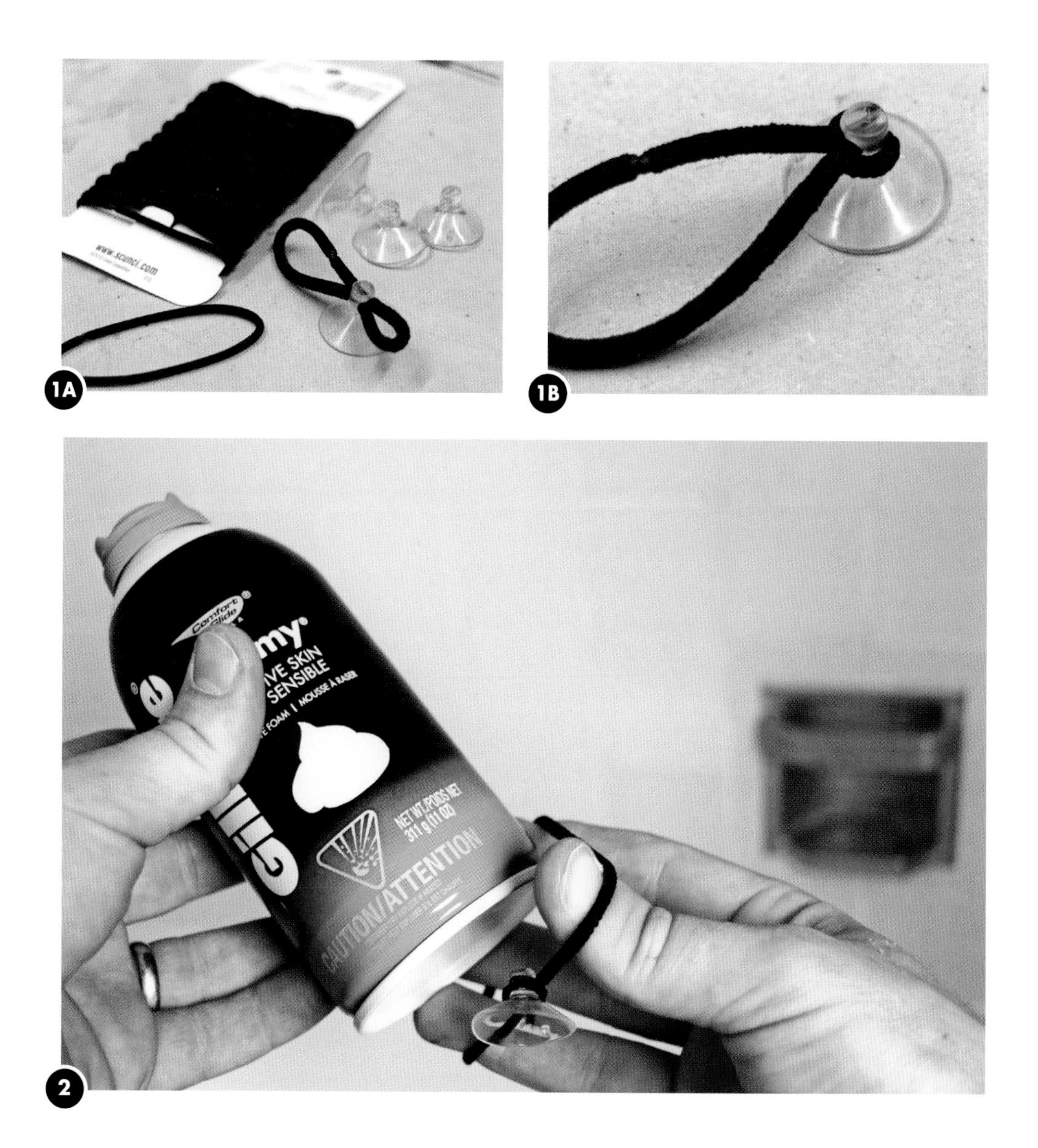

1A and 1B. Small suction cups come in a variety of types. Here, I used suction cups with an opening through the nipple on the back of the cup. Feed a no-metal elastic hair tie through the opening in each suction cup, double back through one end, and cinch it tight, firmly attaching the elastic band to the suction cup.

2. These elastics have a surprising amount of stretch and can accommodate almost any size of bottle you might need in the shower—even shaving cream! Simply stretch the elastic around the bottle, then stick the suction cup to the shower wall at any height you desire.

SWISS ARMY KEYS

MATERIALS AND TOOLS

- KEYS
- MULTITOOL OR CAMPING KNIFE
- DRILL AND BIT TO MATCH RIVET SIZE
- ROTARY TOOL
- EYE PROTECTION
- DUST MASK
- RIVETS AND RIVET SETTER

If you're like me, you don't like feeling like a jailer or custodian with a ring of keys hanging from your hip. Throw your everyday-carry (EDC) multitool into the mix, and now you've got a *really* uncomfortable pocket full of gear. Why not combine your keys and your EDC in a single unit? This project will work with almost any type of multitool. You can also use an inexpensive pocketknife if you (understandably) don't want to break open your favorite knife.

1. The first step is to expose the rivets holding the blades inside the body. You may have to remove plastic or wooden plates to accomplish this.

2. Find the rivet that corresponds to where you want your keys placed. Using a drill bit the same size as the rivet in your knife, drill out the rivet completely, remove all the loose blades, and set them aside. Your pocketknife or multitool should be able to accommodate a key in the slot of each blade or tool you remove.

3. Collect your keys and use a marker to select the areas on the handle tops of the keys you'll need to remove so they'll fit inside the knife body.

4

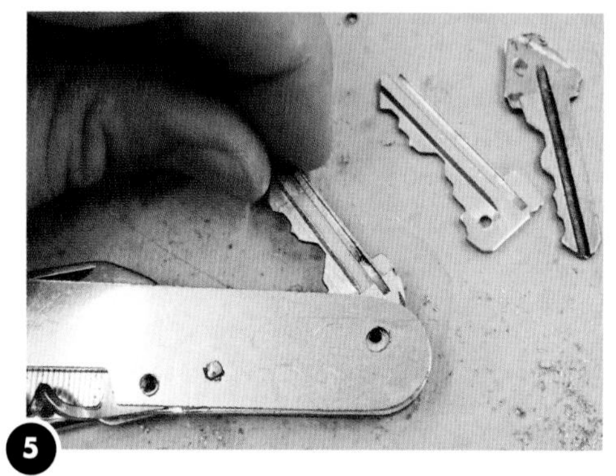

5

6

4. Using a rotary tool, trim the keys where marked. A rotary tool can make lots of metal dust, so wear eye protection and a mask, and work in a well-ventilated area.

5. Test-fit your keys in the knife body and mark where the rivet was so you can locate and mark where to drill the holes in the keys to accommodate the new rivet. Use the same drill bit from before to drill though the trimmed-down key handles.

6. Place the keys into the knife body and feed a new rivet through the body and through the hole drilled into each key. Use the rivet setter to secure the rivet and keys into the knife body. The tail of the rivet will pop off when the rivet is set, so no finishing is required.

TAPE ORGANIZER

MATERIALS AND TOOLS

- SCRAP WOOD
- RULER OR TAPE MEASURE
- PENCIL
- SAW
- HACKSAW BLADE OR OTHER CUTTING EDGE
- WOOD DOWELS
- DRILL AND BIT TO MATCH DOWEL SIZE
- FOUR WOODSCREWS (1½ TO 2 INCHES) FOR FASTENING SIDES TO BASE
- TWO WOODSCREWS (¼ TO ½ INCH) FOR FASTENING BLADE THE SIDES
- SCREWDRIVER BIT

I'm not sure how I end up with so much tape, but it's become a real workshop nuisance. I've tried a few methods of keeping the rolls organized and easily accessible, but I think this is probably the best I've hit upon so far. It isn't the prettiest thing, but this tape organizer keeps the rolls at the ready and even has a blade to help with cutting, which is especially handy when reaching for tape with your one free hand. The rolls are also on a removable dowel, so you can take an entire roll off the organizer when you need to take it elsewhere or when the roll is empty.

1. Using the rolls of tape you want to store as a reference, determine the height of the tape organizer's sides. Because I used an old hacksaw blade as the cutting edge, the distance between the blade's mounting holes determined the final width of the organizer. I used leftover 2×6 project boards I had lying around, but almost any size can work.

2. Drill openings for the dowels in both side pieces, measuring and marking the sides so that the dowels will be relatively level and true from side to side and up and down. I used a ⅝-inch wood dowel, so used a corresponding drill bit for the openings. I positioned the dowel for the small rolls on the top of the organizer in the center of the side boards, but because the larger rolls on the bottom needed more room, I offset the dowel opening toward the rear. I cut the dowel into two sections slightly longer than the entire width of the organizer, allowing for easy grabbing when the dowel needs to be removed.

3. Attach the sides to the base with screws. Place the tape rolls between the sides of the organizer and feed the dowels through the sides to hold the rolls.

4. Install the cutting edge near the bottom of the organizer for the large rolls. You can secure the tape holder to a shelf in almost any orientation.

TENNIS BALL MOUTH HOLDERS

MATERIALS AND TOOLS

- TENNIS BALLS
- HOBBY KNIFE
- LARGE GOOGLY EYES (2 TO 3 MILLIMETERS)
- E6000 ADHESIVE
- SCREWS AND LARGE WASHERS

These goofy holders made from tennis balls are as cute as they are functional. They are a great way to add character to your workshop or home and they can hold a surprising array of items—keys, notes, small hand tools, and just about anything else that will fit in their mouths!

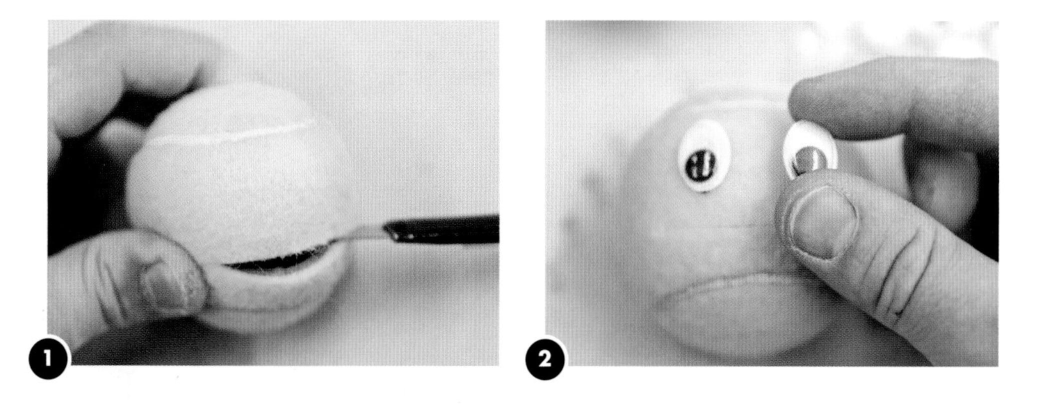

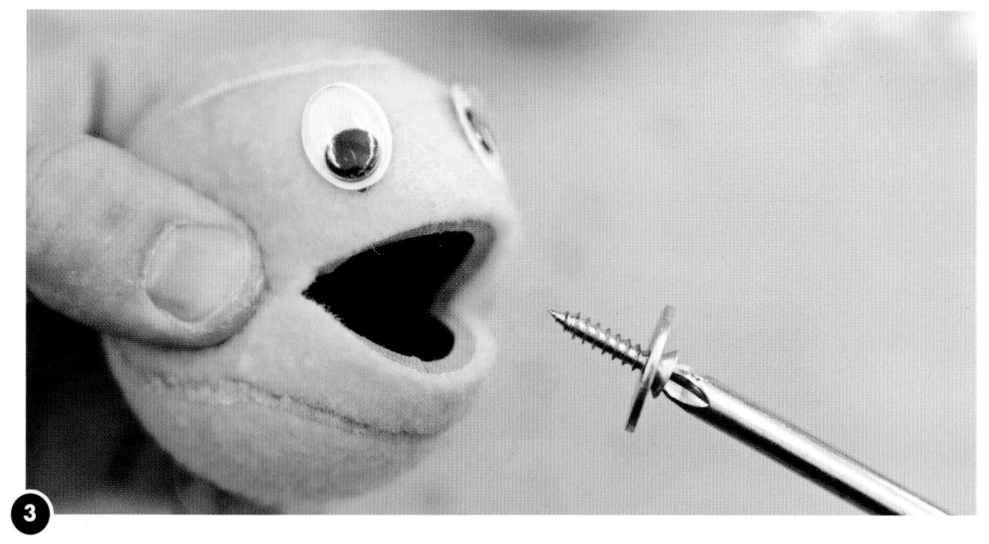

1. Start by making the mouth. Using a sharp hobby knife, carefully slice an opening about 2 inches long. Make the cut on the side of the ball opposite the logo so that it doesn't show after the holder is mounted. The most difficult part is to get the cut started, so use extra care when making the initial cut, and always cut away from yourself!

2. Once you've made the cut, add the googly eyes. Use E6000 or another strong glue so they don't come off.

3. Pushing on the sides of the incision causes the mouth to open and allows you to insert a screw with a large washer inside, thus affixing the tennis ball to any sturdy surface. The large washer distributes the pressure from the screw on the inside of the tennis ball and prevents the tennis from being pulled off the mounting surface.

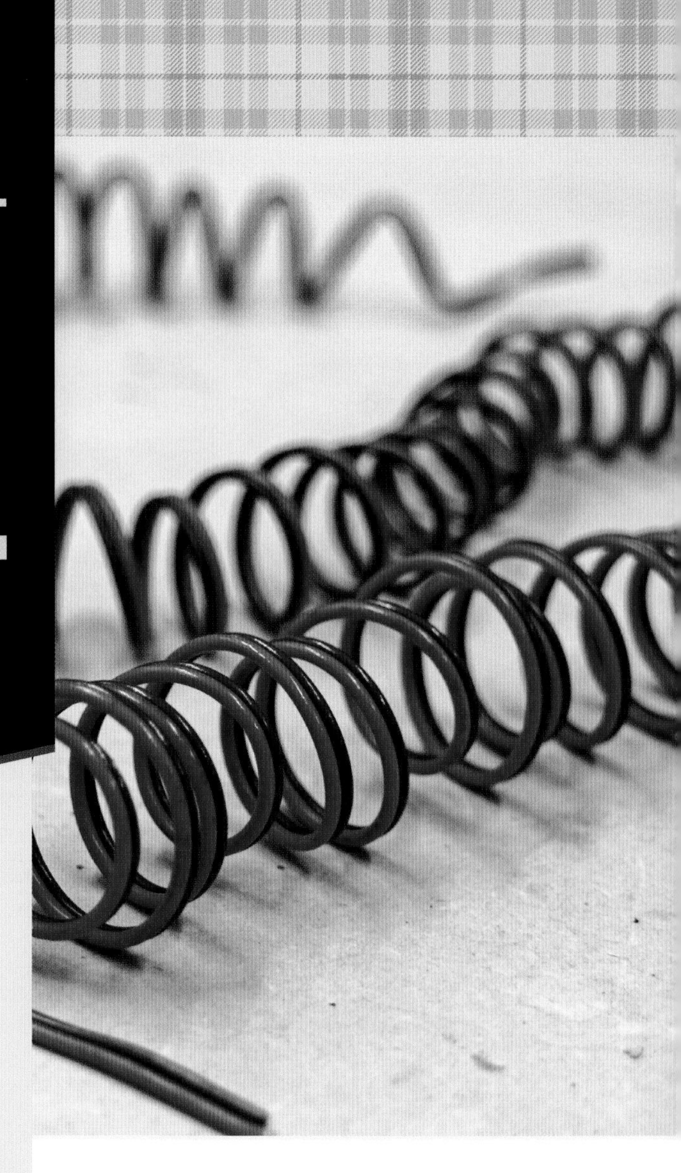

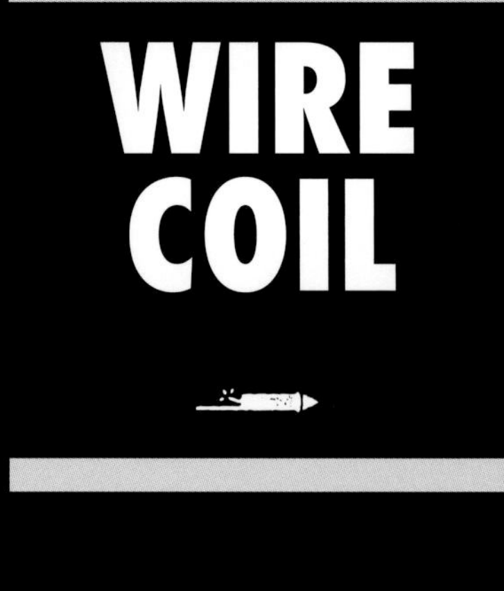

WIRE COIL

MATERIALS AND TOOLS

- WIRE WITH A VINYL JACKET
- DOWEL OR METAL ROD
- ELECTRICAL TAPE
- HEAT GUN
- CLAMP
- DRILL

If you've ever done any electrical work, you know how easy it is to end up with a tangled mess of wires on your hands. This project is a great way to keep things organized, and you can do it yourself without having to spend big bucks at the store.

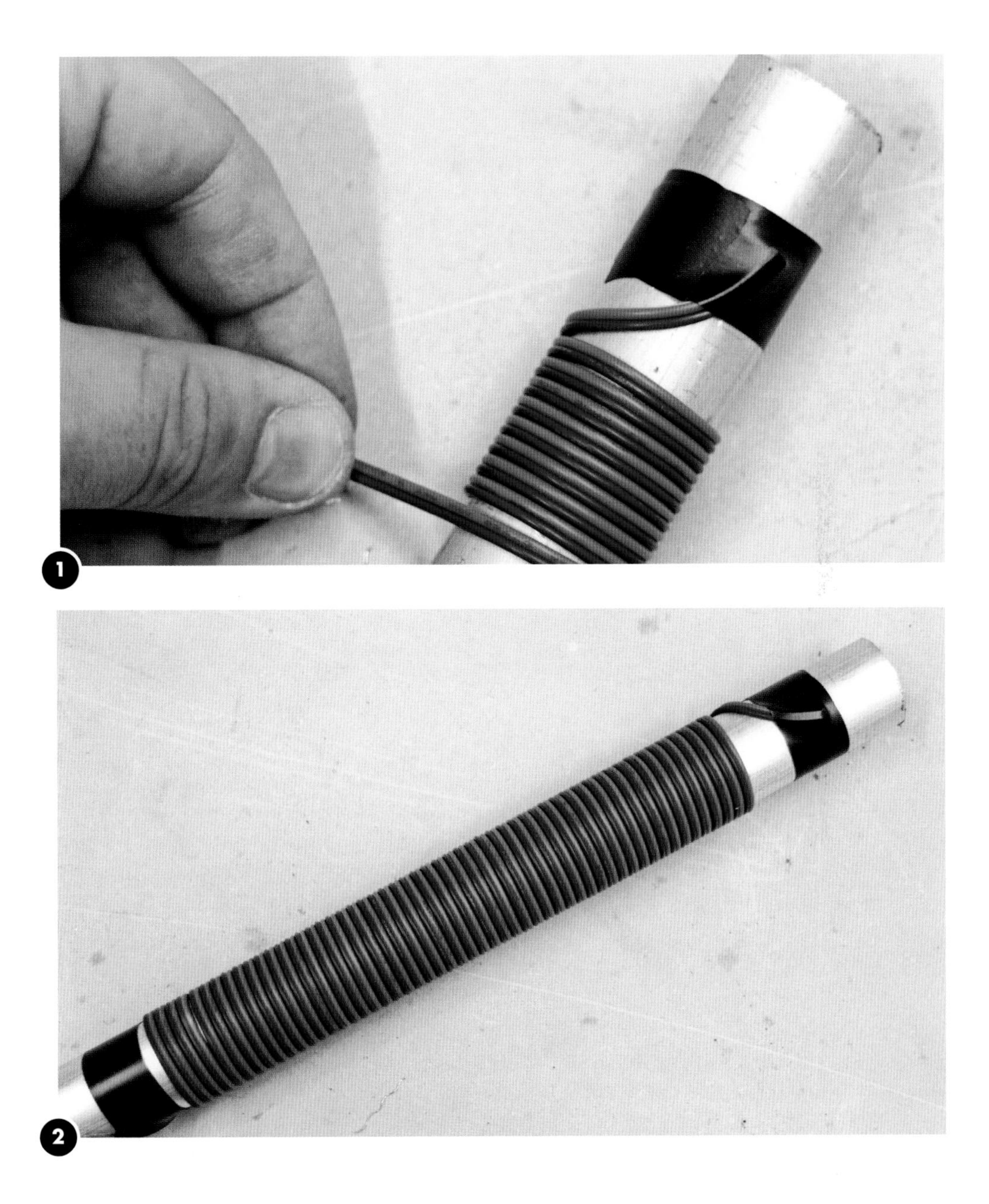

1. Tape one end of your wire to the end of a dowel (or rod) and then manually wrap the wire around it, taking the time to make sure the wire is tightly wrapped flat against the dowel with no spacing between wraps.

2. Secure the second end of the wire with more tape.

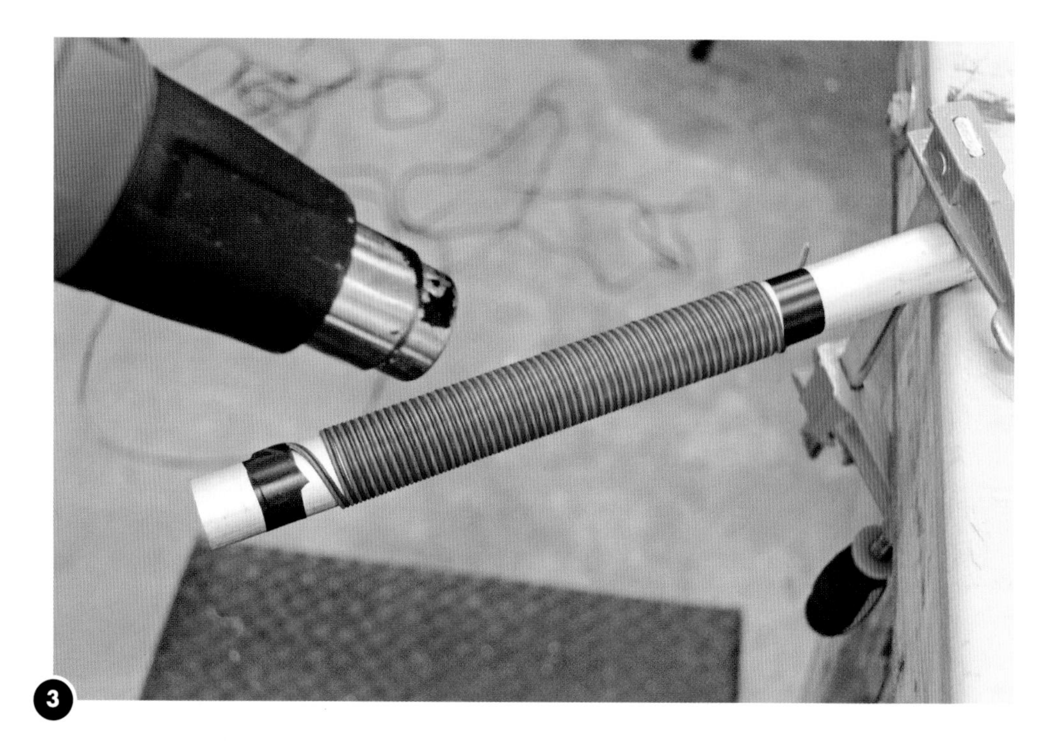

3. Set your heat gun to a low setting and gently heat up the wires, waving the nozzle around the wrapped wire so as not to burn or melt the wire's vinyl jacket. The heat gun will soften the vinyl, allowing it relax and take on the shape of the dowel. After a few minutes, you'll see the jacket start to turn glossy; this is when you know you've hit the right temperature. Turn off the heat gun and allow the vinyl to cool.

4. Remove the tape and slide the wrapped wire off the dowel or rod. You could leave the wire in the loose coil, but to make this coiled wire nice and tight we'll reverse the coiling direction.

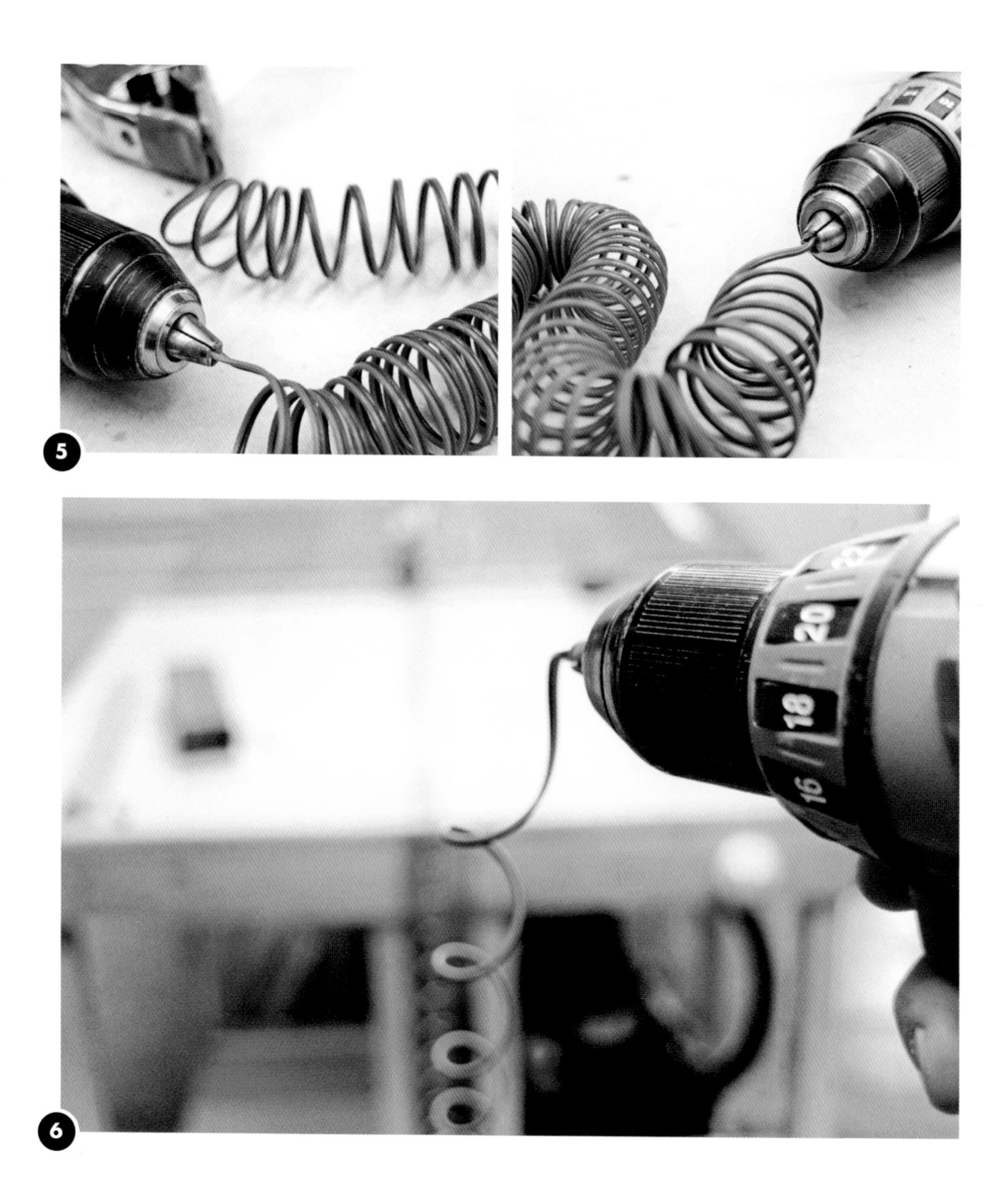

5. Clamp one end of the coiled wire to the workbench and insert the other end into the chuck of your drill. If your wire is coiled clockwise then you'll need your drill set to go counterclockwise, and vice versa.

6. Engage the drill and the coil will reverse direction one loop at a time. Reversing the coiling after heating the vinyl jacket tightens the coiling and makes the wire much neater. Remove the wire from the workbench and drill and clip any ends of wire damaged from clamping. Your coiled wire is now ready for use in your project.

WRENCH COAT HOOKS

MATERIALS AND TOOLS

- **COMBINATION WRENCHES**
- **PROPANE TORCH**
- **BENCH VISE**
- **DRILL AND COUNTERSINK**
- **LOCKING PLIERS**
- **HEAVY-DUTY SCRUBBING PADS**
- **SCREWS FOR MOUNTING**

Coat hooks might seem like mighty fancy home accessories, but the truth is your man cave needs a place for you to hang your pants after a long day in the shop. In addition to being functional, these industrial coat hooks made from combination wrenches are a great way to accent your wall.

Almost any combination wrench will work for this project, but smaller sizes are easier to bend than those really beefy wrenches, so gather your materials accordingly. The torch will heat up the steel wrenches, changing their molecular structure. As the hardened steel loses its temper, you be able to drill and bend it without the need for heavy shop machinery.

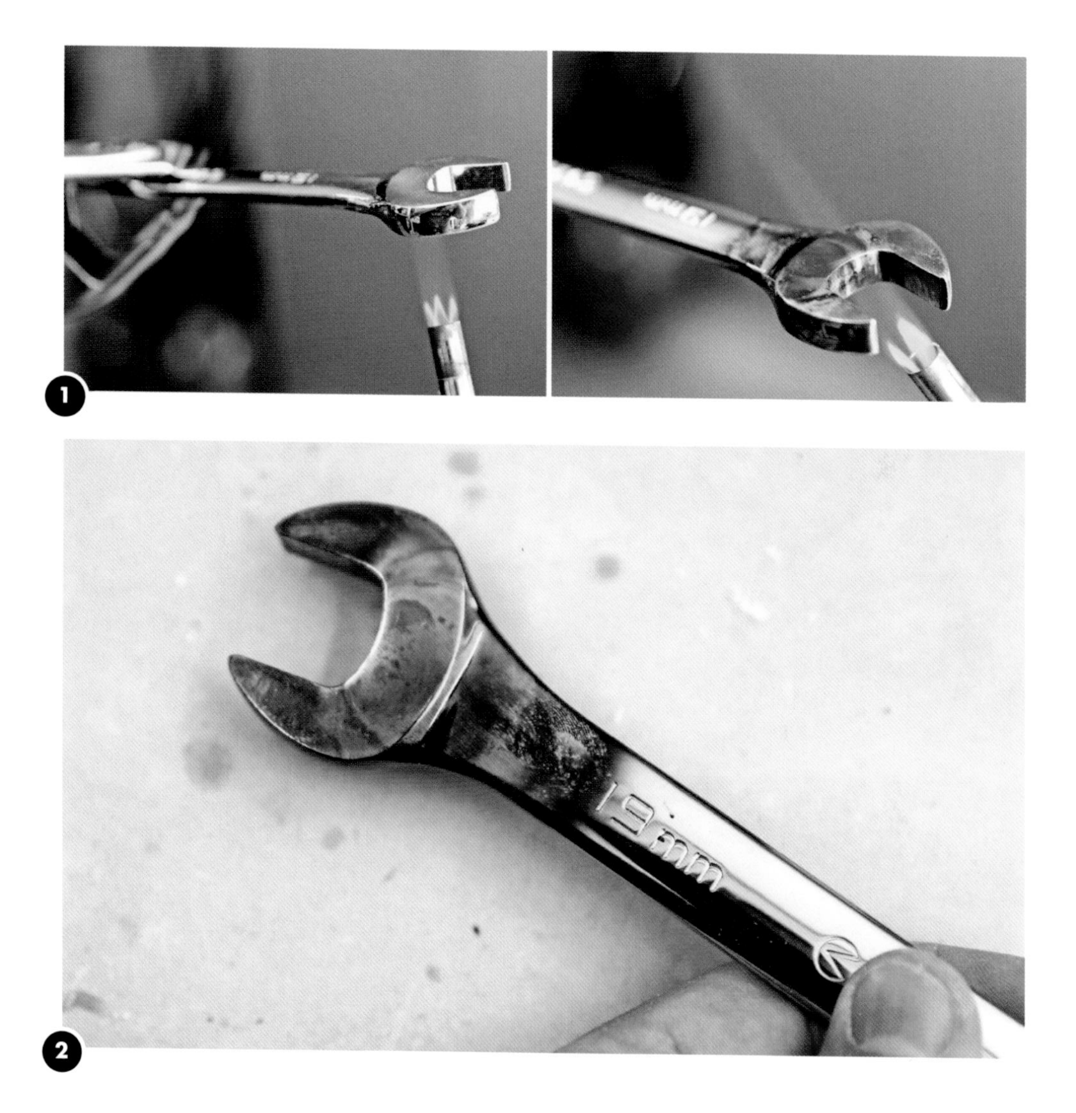

1. Start by holding your wrench in a clamp with the head protruding so you can heat up the wrench without heating the clamp (and burning your fingers). Place your propane torch so the tip of the flame lands on the surface of the wrench. The torch should heat the area where you want the mounting hole to be.

2. After a few minutes the area should turn bright red. Allow the steel to air-cool completely before attempting to drill.

3

3. When the torch is cool to the touch, there should be obvious signs of discoloration; this is good. Using a regular bit, drill an opening through the wrench head. The steel should be soft enough to drill through with downward pressure. Finish the hole with a countersink to accommodate the screw head's taper.

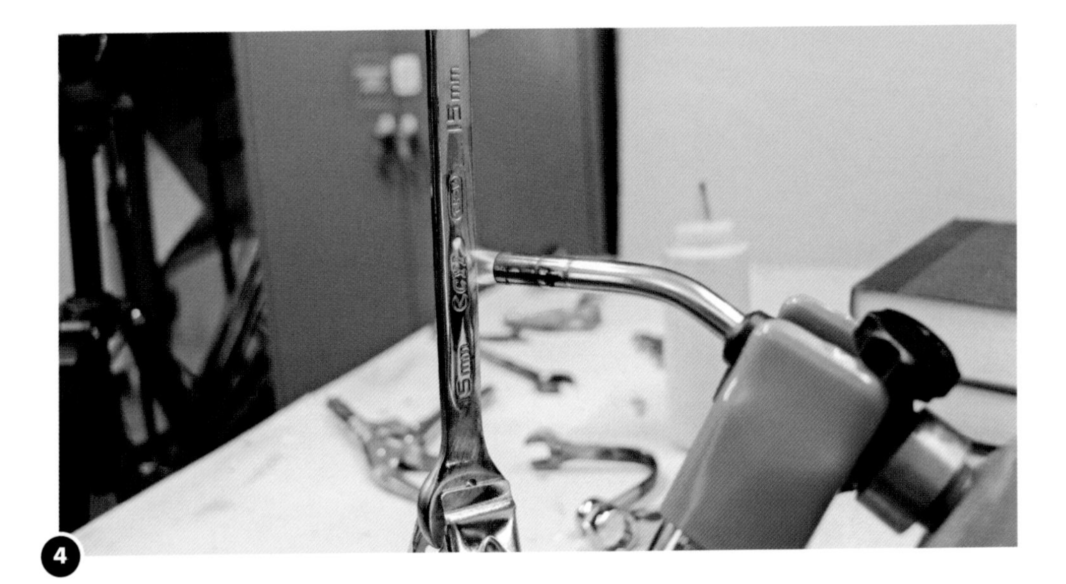

4

4. To bend the wrenches into hooks, you'll work the steel while it's hot. Clamp the drilled wrenches and heat up the middle area of the wrench handle. After a few minutes the wrench will begin to glow. This is when you know the wrench is ready to be bent.

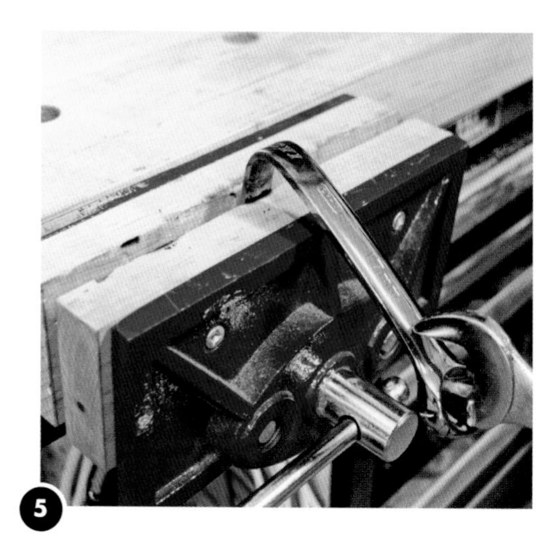
5

6

7

5. While the wrench is still red hot, move it into a bench vice and clamp it down tightly. Using locking pliers, pull the wrench forward to make a bend at the heated area. With my combination wrenches, I found I could easily use another wrench in the closed end of the clamped wrench to gain leverage for an easy bend. Allow the wrench to cool before removing.

6. After you've bent your wrenches, the discoloration can be cleaned up with any tough scouring pad and a few minutes of elbow grease. If you have air tools and conditioning discs, this job can be done even more quickly.

7. Your bent wrenches are ready to be mounted anywhere you need an industrial hook.

-DUDE CRAFTS-
STYLISH
LIVING

CANDLE BOTTLE TOPPERS

MATERIALS AND TOOLS

- **STIFF COPPER WIRE (12 GAUGE OR SIMILAR)**
- **SILICONE BOTTLE STOPPERS**
- **HOBBY KNIFE**
- **BALING WIRE**
- **DRILL WITH ⅛-INCH BIT**
- **TEA LIGHTS**
- **WIRE SNIPS**

Few things are more enjoyable than a late-night beverage outside under the stars. The only thing better is when it's with company, and this project definitely ups the romantic ambience in your outdoor space. What happens while (or after) you imbibe your nightcap is up to you.

The top of the bottle is used as a stand for the stiff wires that hold the tea lights. Copper wire can be found among lots of discarded wire. Check your local recycling depot.

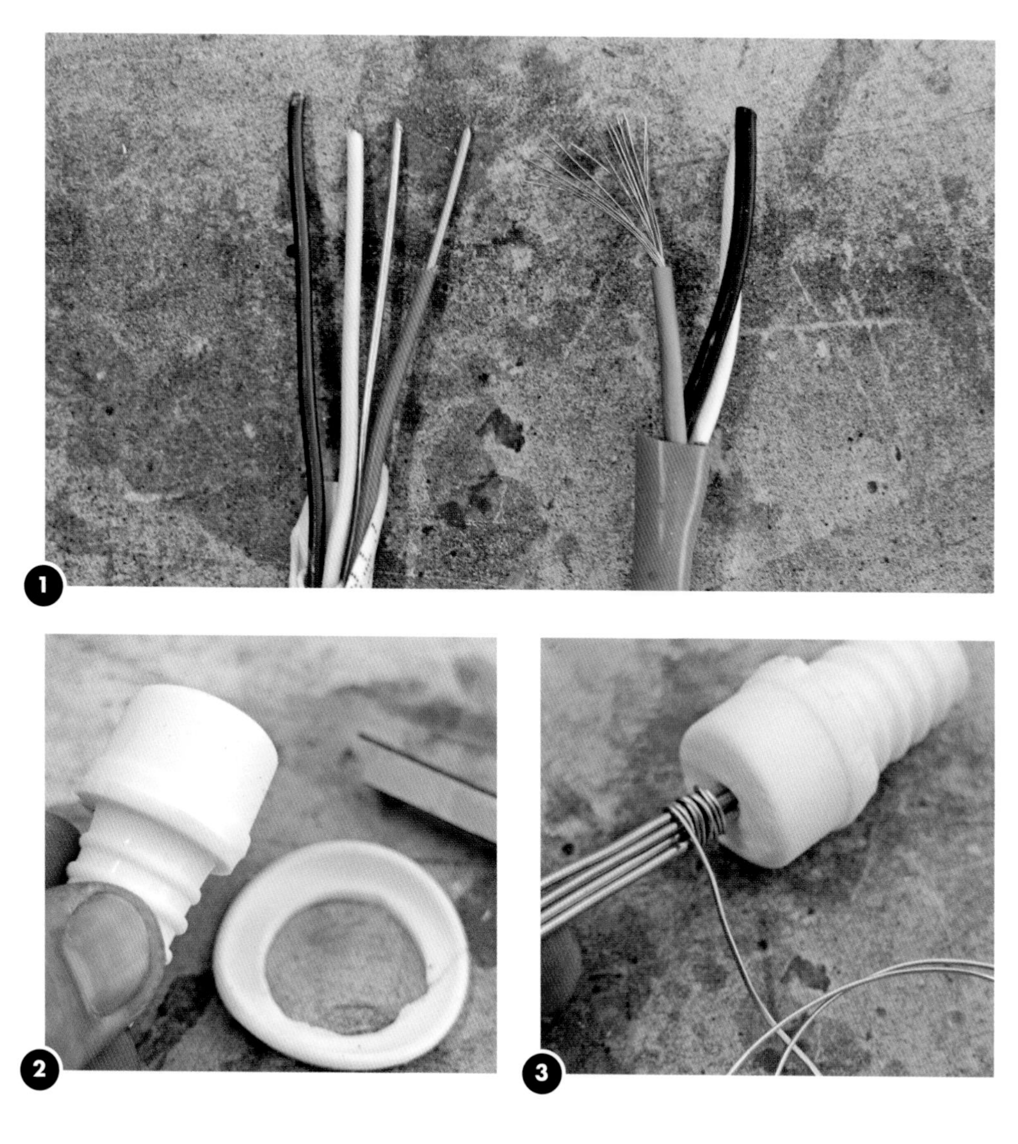

1. If the wire has a vinyl jacket, strip this to reveal the copper wires inside. Cut four segments of wire, each about 12 inches in length.

2. Use a hobby knife to remove the flange from the silicone stopper.

3. Use baling wire to secure the copper wire segments together. Drill a small opening into the silicone cork and insert the bundle of copper wires.

4. Bend the wires outward to make arms radiating from the cork. Use the circumference of the tea lights to form the copper wire ends into cradles that will hold the tea lights.

5. Use a small section of baling wire to secure each copper wire cradle closed.

6. Use your artistic expression to make the cradles any shapes you like.

7. Place the cork into your bottle of wine and add tealights to each cradle. Since the copper wire is still bendy, you can make any modifications you deem necessary at any time. Light up the candles, grab your date, and let the good times roll.

CONCRETE-BALLOON CANDLE HOLDERS

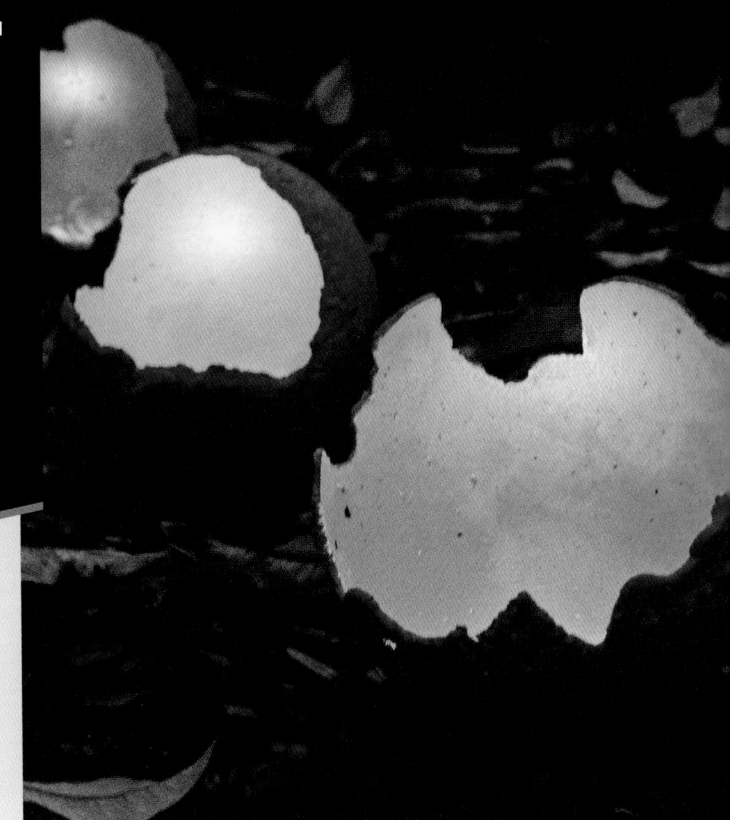

MATERIALS AND TOOLS

- CONCRETE MIX
- RUBBER GLOVES AND DUST MASK
- WIRE COLANDER
- PLASTIC CONTAINER
- PAPER CUP
- BALLOONS
- DUCT TAPE
- SMALL TROWEL
- METALLIC ACRYLIC CRAFT PAINT
- SPONGE BRUSH
- TEA LIGHTS

The balance of strength and fragility in these concrete-balloon candle holders makes them a conversation starter and functional accessory for your next evening backyard event.

When working with concrete, always wear proper protection, including gloves and a dust mask, as well as older clothes. Concrete is alkaline (on the opposite end of the pH spectrum from acid) and can cause burns on skin. If you get any concrete on your skin, flush with plenty of water to neutralize and wash it away.

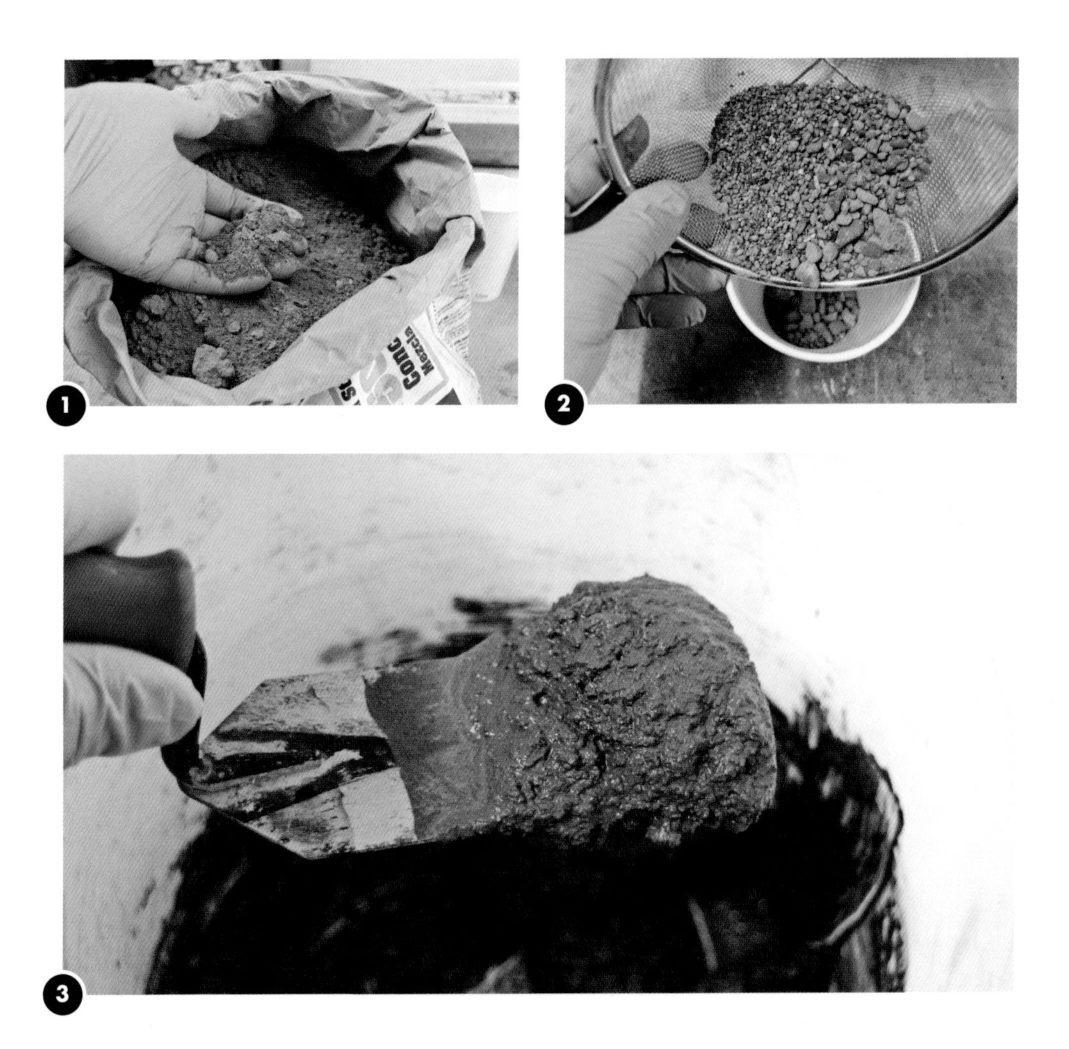

1. Concrete is available in all kinds of mixes, incorporating various additives and aggregate (stone) sizes. Aggregate is used in concrete to increase the compressive strength and add volume to the mix. Since you don't need either of these attributes for this project, you can use a mix that has very small aggregate, like countertop mix. Or simply use a wire colander to remove the aggregate from any type of store-bought concrete.

2. If you do remove aggregate, save it in a paper cup; this will be used later as a weighted stand to hold the balloon. Alternately, you can use sand or some other weighty material.

3. Add a small amount of water to the sifted concrete to make a mix, roughly three parts concrete to one part water—you're looking for a very dry porridge consistency. Mix the concrete with a small trowel in a plastic container, ensuring all pockets of dry concrete mix have been completely mixed with water.

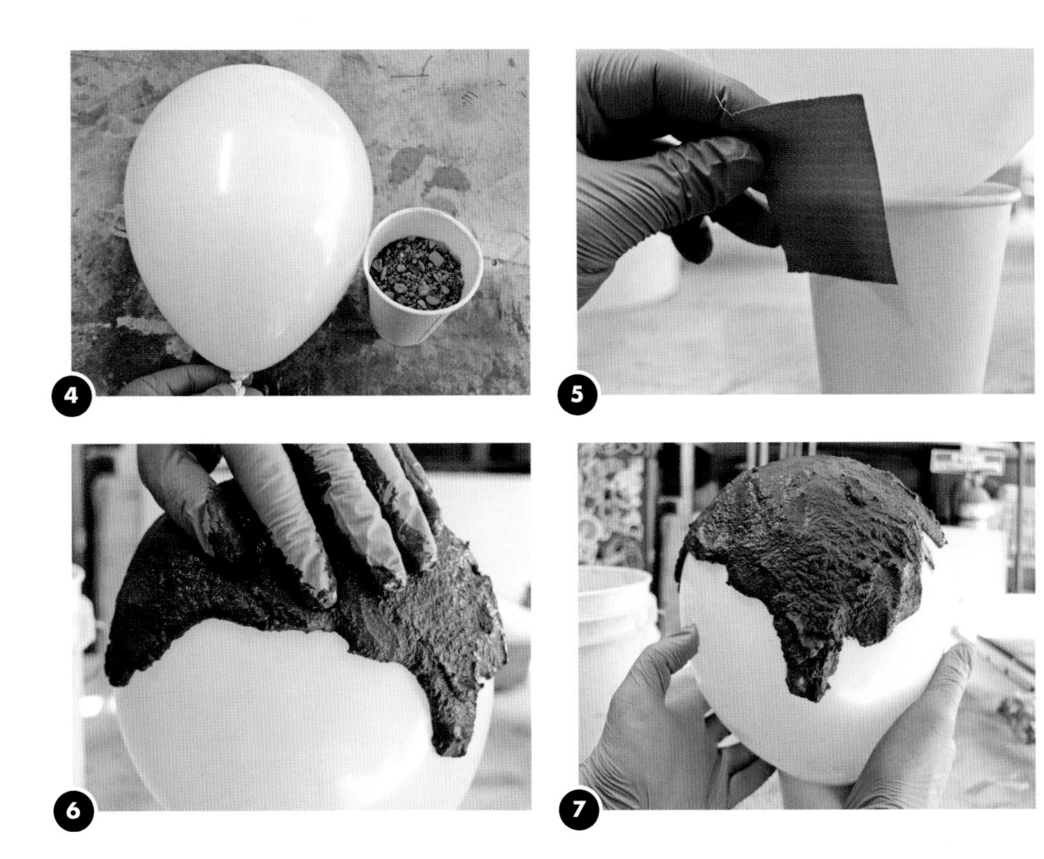

4. Blow up a balloon to whatever size you like, then place it on the open mouth of the paper cup weighted with the sieved aggregate or sand.

5. Use a large square of duct tape to secure the balloon to the cup.

6. With your gloved hands, scoop a small amount of mixed concrete onto the top of the balloon. Continue adding small handfuls of concrete, gently spreading it over the balloon's surface in an even coat.

7. Once you've covered the top half of the balloon, stop and examine your work to determine if there are areas where the concrete is too thin or dropping off the bottom. Gently push the concrete around to get the shape you want. Imperfection looks good on these forms, so don't sweat it. Set the balloon cast aside to cure overnight.

8

9

10

8. After 24 hours the concrete will be cured and can be handled. Remove the balloon from the cup and gently set it on your work surface so the concrete-covered portion is on the table and the exposed balloon is facing upward. Pierce the balloon to pop it.

9. Gently wipe the inside of the balloon casting with a damp paper towel.

10. To really make the insides shine, brush on a metallic acrylic paint and allow to dry for a few hours. The last step is to put a tea light inside the concrete balloon and set it outside. A few of these make for a striking arrangement in your garden. Because they are thin, these projects are fragile, so handle with care. Luckily, making replacements is easy!

KINTSUGI

MATERIALS AND TOOLS

- BROKEN POTTERY
- TWO-PART EPOXY
- METALLIC PIGMENT POWDER
- CRAFT STICKS
- PAINTER'S TAPE (OPTIONAL)

Kintsugi is the Japanese art of repairing broken pottery using an adhesive mixed with a shiny metallic pigment. Simply put, the philosophy behind kintsugi is the acceptance of flaws, change, and fate, which reflect life events.

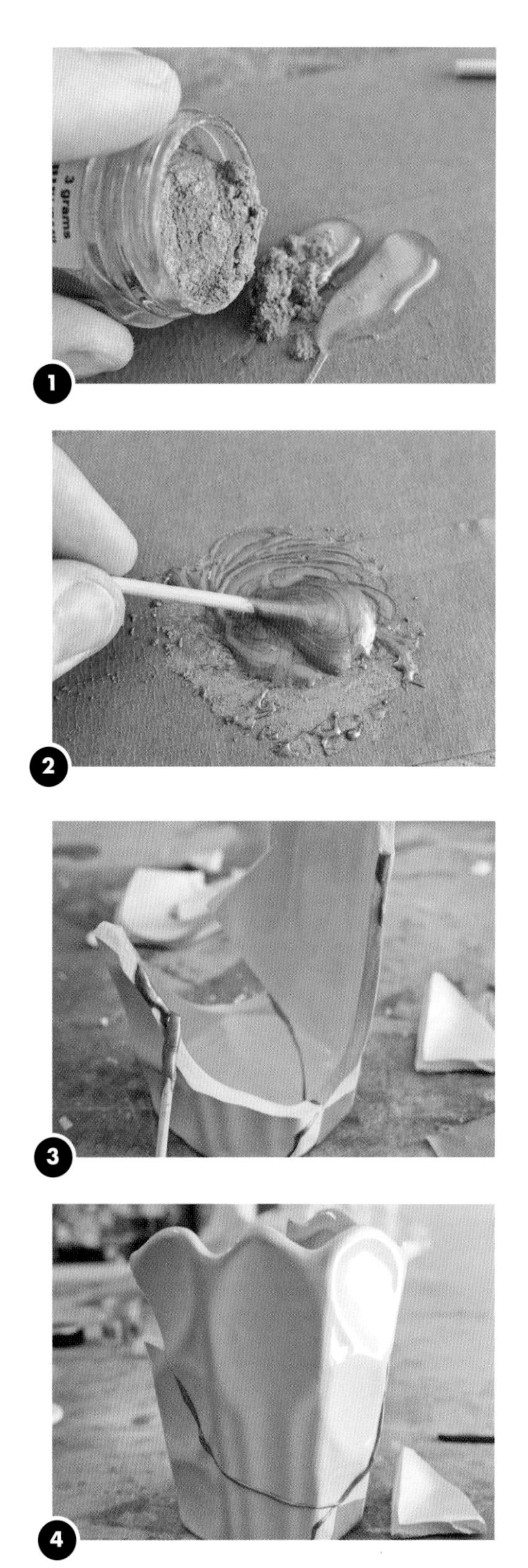

1. To repair broken pottery, you'll need a strong adhesive, like a two-part epoxy. Squeeze out the epoxy onto a mixing surface. Before mixing the epoxy resin with the hardener, scoop some metallic powder into the epoxy parts. These pigment powders can be found in any craft store or online.

2. With the powder pigment added, thoroughly mix the epoxy with a craft stick, bamboo skewer, or other disposable implement until the two parts are completely combined and there are no lumps of pigment powder.

3. Once the metallic epoxy is mixed, you need to work quickly, as the pot life of epoxy can be very short. Carefully dab a liberal amount of epoxy onto a broken edge of the pottery and then join it with its adjacent piece.

4. It can help to use painter's tape to hold sections together while the epoxy cures, though allowing the epoxy/pigment mixture to squeeze out between the adhered pieces can add to the aesthetic appeal of kintsugi.

MAGNETIC **CEILING STORAGE**

MATERIALS AND TOOLS

- **STRONG MAGNETS**
- **SCREWDRIVER (IF NEEDED)**
- **NUTS AND WASHERS**
- **NEEDLE AND THREAD**
- **PARACORD**
- **HEAT-SHRINK TUBING (OPTIONAL)**

After a hard day of work, you could keep your everyday carry (EDC) in a bowl by the door, but it's sometimes hard to see (and remember) whether you actually placed your keys in the bowl. A magnetic storage solution not only keeps your EDC tidy and out of the way but also allows you to see at a glance whether you've stowed your things away. This magnetic storage doesn't have to be on the ceiling—it works just as well on a door or under a desk.

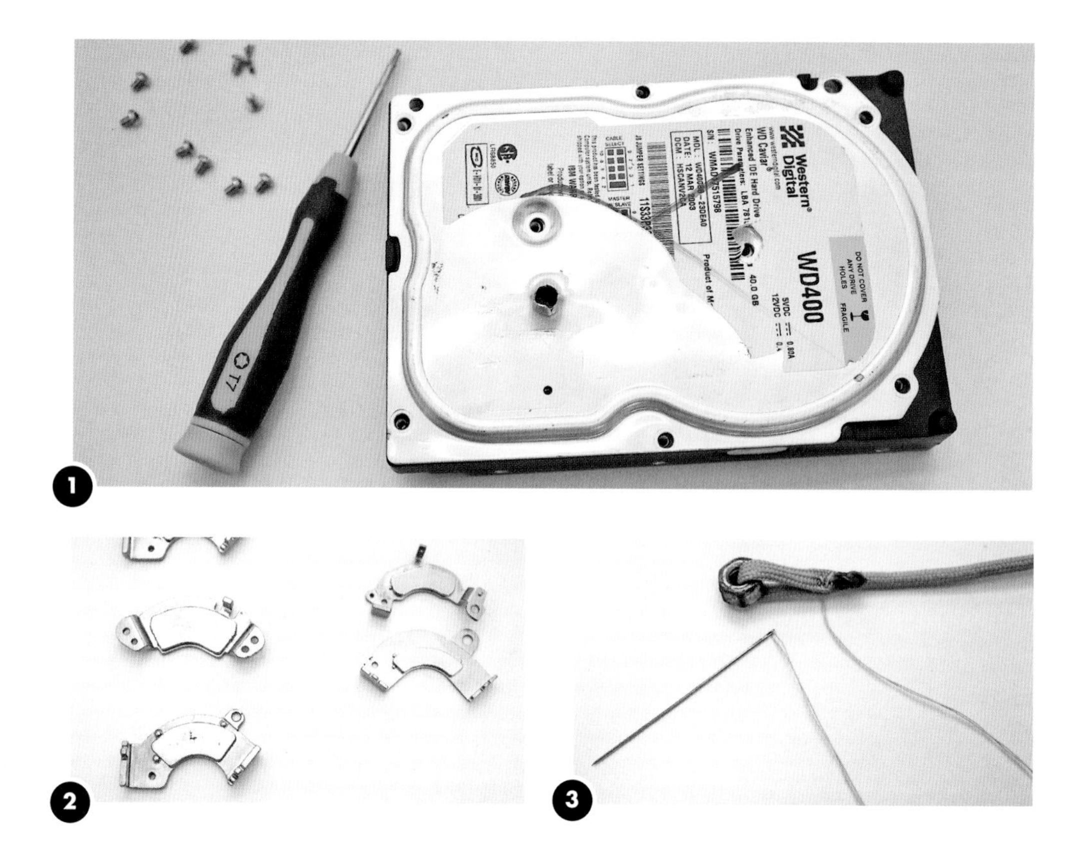

1. You can buy strong magnets, but you can also easily find them inside almost all discarded electronics that have motors. Old computer hard drives have very powerful magnets inside that can be removed and repurposed in a few different ways. I used them in this project as magnetic attachment plates.

Use a small screwdriver to remove the hard-drive casing screws. Carefully remove the hard-drive platters until you find the curved magnet near the bottom. These magnets aren't usually held in place with much more than some retaining clips and can easily be pulled out.

2. Once removed, the magnets from the hard drive are conveniently already mounted to steel mounting brackets with pre-drilled holes. This makes remounting the powerful magnets anywhere else a breeze.

3. To allow your EDC items to attach easily to this strong magnet, you'll need to ensure there's ferrous metal somewhere on whatever it is you want to stick to the magnet. Keys, for example, will likely attach at their keyring. For my wallet, which doesn't have ferrous metal on it, I used a nut attached by a length of paracord. Some care needs to be taken here, as strong magnets can corrupt the black magnetic strips on the backs of credit cards. I looped a small section of paracord through a steel nut and sewed it closed.

4. Use a tube of heat-shrink tubing to cover the stitches and provide a tidy look.

5. Sew the paracord and nut to the fold of the wallet.

6. You're not limited to just wallet and keys with this project! I sewed a stainless-steel-coated washer inside my hat, which will allow me to hand-wash my hat without the washer rusting. The washer provides more than enough ferrous surface to allow the hat to hang from the magnet.

This simple solution is a fun way to store your EDC or anything else you readily need to take with you. It works equally well in the shop for holding tools and at home for your keys, wallet, pocketknife, and more.

SINGLE-FLOWER VASE

MATERIALS AND TOOLS

- **INEXPENSIVE SMALL WOODEN BOWL**
- **SMALL JAR WITH LID**
- **THICK-STEMMED FLOWER (LIKE A DAISY OR LILY)**
- **TWO-PART EPOXY**

A bouquet of flowers is always nice, but chances are your significant other has a favorite type of flower they really like. Instead of relying on a mixed assortment from the corner grocery store to tell them you care, show them you're *really* paying attention by giving them exactly what they want. Besides, by now they've probably earned something nice for putting up with you if you've attempted any of the other projects in this book!

1. For this example, I used an inexpensive wooden salad bowl from IKEA, but the thrift store is a great (and even cheaper) place to source items like this. Find a small jar with lid that fits completely underneath the bowl—the jar needs to be shorter than the inside height of the upside-down bowl.

2. Find a thick-stemmed flower that your partner is partial to, then choose a drill bit slightly larger than the typical diameter of the flower stem

3. Drill an opening in the center of the bowl's bottom.

4. Drill a corresponding opening in the jar lid.

5. Remove any sharp metal burrs before epoxying the lid to the inside bottom of the bowl. Allow the epoxy to cure overnight.

6. Partially fill the glass jar with water and screw the jar onto the lid inside the overturned bowl. Then cut the flower to length and insert in the opening in the bowl. This simple and elegant vase is a fun and different way to showcase a flower.

STRING LAMP

MATERIALS AND TOOLS

- WHITE GLUE
- PAPER CUP
- YARN
- SCISSORS
- BALLOON
- DROP CLOTH
- LIGHT SOCKET AND LAMP CORD

String lamps can cost loads of money if you buy them in the store, especially the larger ones. Happily, not only is making your own one of the easiest projects in this book, but you can make them in any size or color to suit your tastes. Regular round party balloons work well for most rooms, but if you have a spacious lounging area that requires a large string lamp you'll need to source a large balloon, perhaps from a party-supply store. Whichever size you choose, the process is the same.

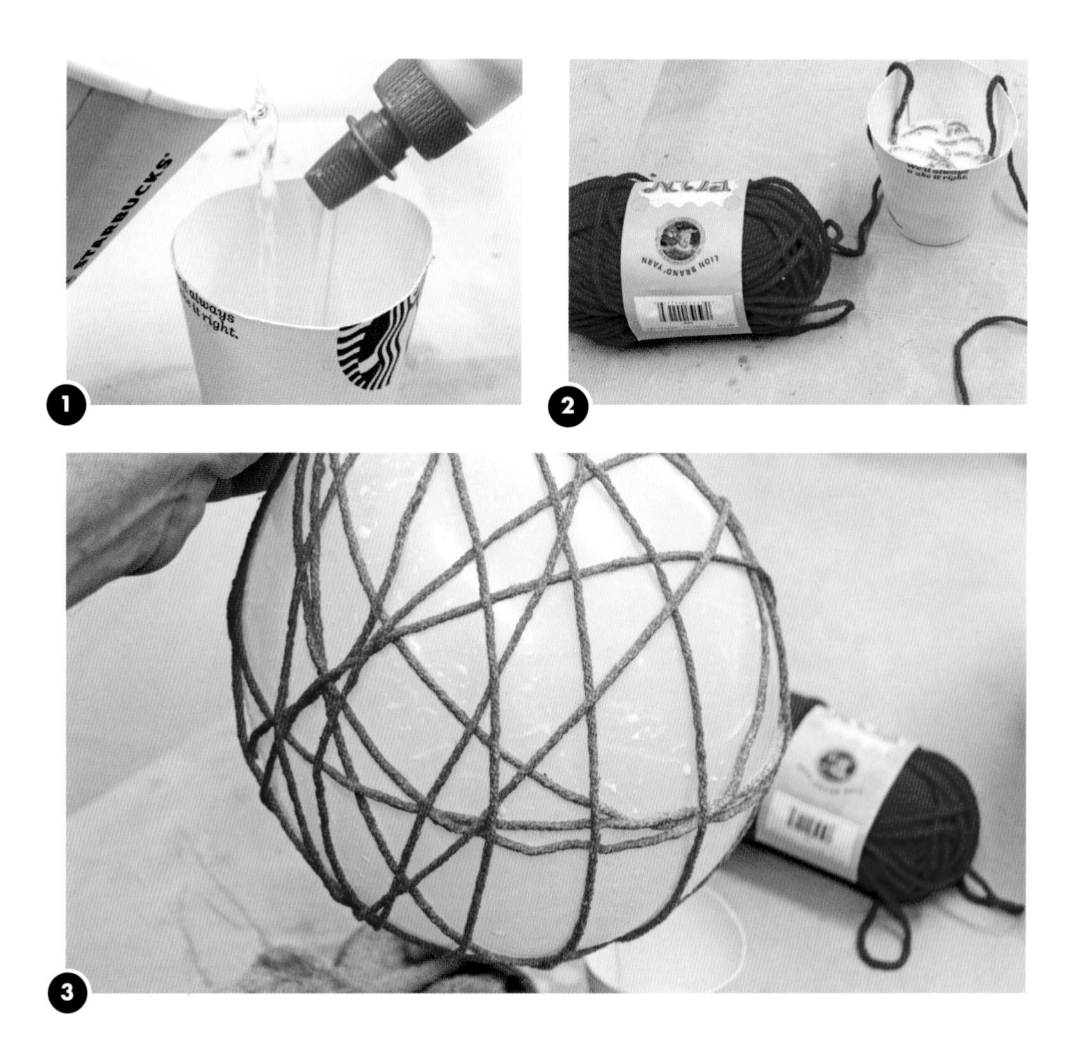

1. Pour white glue into a paper cup and thin it out with a little water. You'll be using quite a bit of yarn, so a 16- or 20-ounce coffee cup works well. You want the glue to be less viscous than normal, so it will easily soak into the yarn, but not so watery that it doesn't set stiffly (or takes a long time to set). I used about a glue-to-water ratio of about ten parts to one.

2. Unravel approximately 20 to 30 feet of yarn and dunk it into the paper cup of glue mixture. Work it around in the cup to completely saturate the yarn.

3. While the yarn is soaking, blow up your balloon and tie it off. Take the end of the saturated yarn and make a few turns around the balloon's knot to prevent the yarn from slipping off, then begin wrapping yarn around the entire balloon, varying the wrap routes slightly to maximize yarn coverage. When you're out of yarn, tuck the end under one of the wrappings to hold it in place. If you want even more yarn coverage, simply dunk more yarn into the glue mixture and keep wrapping until your balloon has achieved the look you like. You can even try a couple of colors together.

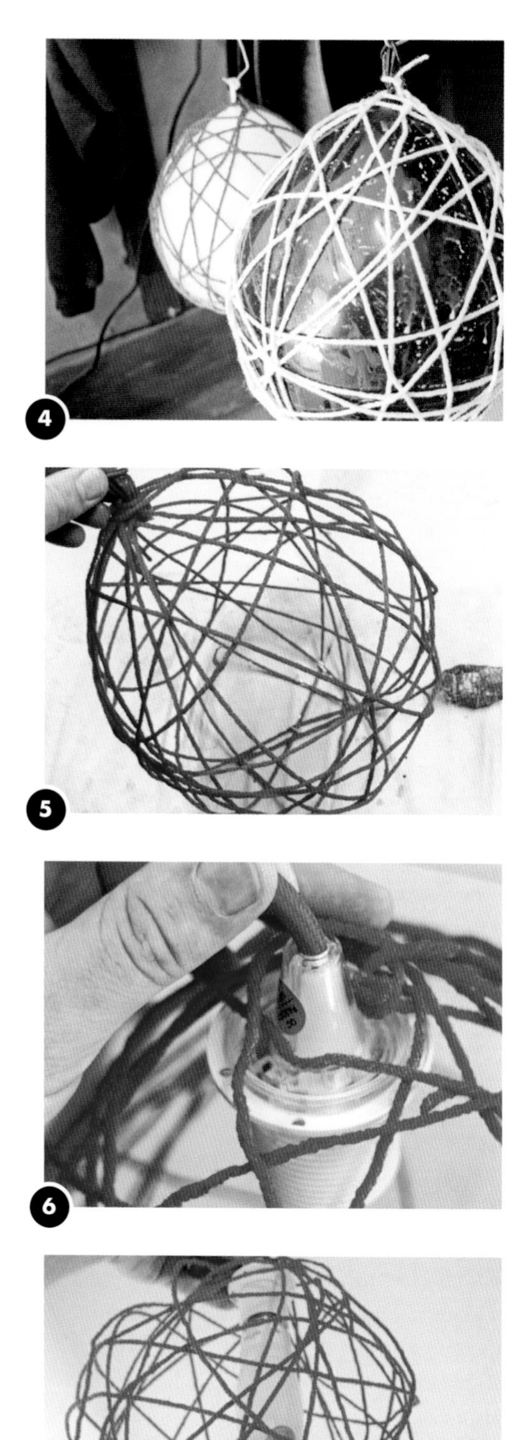

4. Hang the balloon until the glue hardens, placing a drop cloth underneath it to catch any glue drippings. Temperature is critical to the drying, since the balloon will shrink in cooler air and cause the string lamp to implode. A good option is to hang your lamp to dry in direct sunlight for about an hour; the balloon won't deflate, and the sun rays help dry the glue quickly.

5. When the glue has dried completely, pop the balloon and carefully remove it from inside the string lamp.

6. The former location of the balloon knot is a good place to install the light socket. You can usually rearrange or possibly cut away some of the overlapping yarn to accommodate the socket.

7. Screw in your bulb and hang your string lamp. For an added bit of class, use a fancy bulb, since it will be fully exposed.

TOY CAR SHOOTERS

MATERIALS AND TOOLS

- DIE-CAST TOY CARS
- SHOT GLASSES
- TWO-PART EPOXY
- CRAFT STICKS
- TOWEL
- HEAVY SCREWDRIVER
- DRILL WITH BITS TO SIZE (IF NEEDED)

Drinking and driving is never okay—unless you're operating one of these toy cars while under the influence. Pair your favorite cars with novelty shot glasses to create unique combinations for guests or to give as presents.

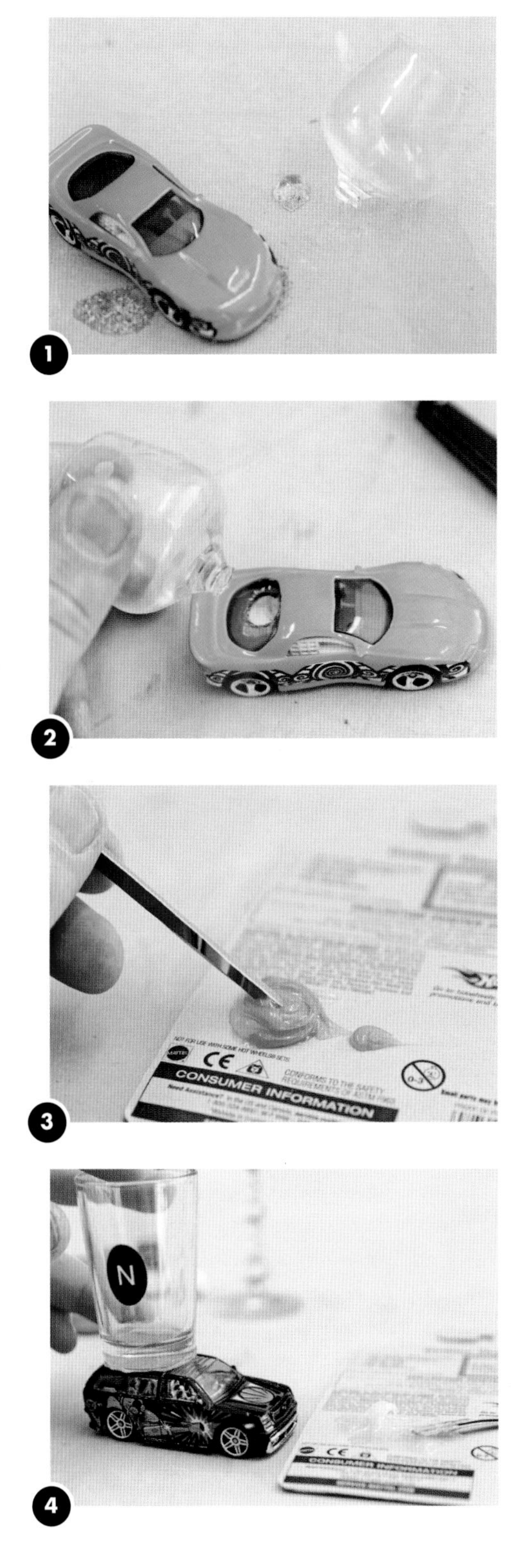

1. The best cars and shot glasses for this project will have flat areas where a good bond can be made. If that's what you've got, skip directly to step 3! If not, read on: Some fancy aperitif glasses have unique shapes or stems; the latter need to be removed before mounting. In this case, wrap the glassware in a towel and gently tap with a screwdriver at the stem to break the glass as close to the bowl of the glass as possible. Don't worry if the break isn't clean, as it will be buried inside the hole you drill.

2. For fancy glasses and cars with curved tops, the toy car can be modified to accept this tapered bottom by drilling a hole in which to insert the taper.

3. Mix your epoxy with a craft stick or other disposable tool.

4. For flat-bottomed glasses and toy cars that have flat tops, simply clean any debris from the bonding surfaces and adhere the two parts using your two-part epoxy. For fancy glasses, insert the tapered stem in the drilled hole and bond with epoxy.

Allow all epoxy to cure overnight before using. Clean the glassware thoroughly before using.

VINYL RECORD BOWL

MATERIALS AND TOOLS

- **12-INCH VINYL RECORD**
- **OVEN-SAFE MIXING BOWL**
- **OVEN**
- **OVEN MITTS**

Collecting vinyl has never been more hip. But for every good record there are hundreds that no one will ever listen to again. Don't believe me? Check out your neighborhood thrift store. Save these retro recordings from the landfill and give them a new life as bowls that make great additions to the home of any music fan in your life. For extra points, try finding records that match the person or function for which the bowls are intended. For example, a calypso record might make a good fruit bowl, or a kids' record might make a great bowl for holding stuffed animals. Happy melting!

1. You can buy records at any thrift store or yard sale, usually with the spare change in your pocket. With a suitable donor record in hand, find an oven-safe bowl, ideally with a diameter no larger than two-thirds that of the record.

2. Invert the bowl in the center rack of your oven and turn the oven on to a low temperature (about 250°F or 120°C).

3. When the oven and your bowl are warmed up, center your record on top of the upside-down bowl and place them in the oven.

4. Close the oven and watch carefully; in less than a minute the vinyl will start to sag and drop around the bowl. When your desired shape is achieved, turn off the oven. Don't leave the record in the oven for more than three minutes, or you will risk melting the record entirely and having a smelly mess to clean up.

5. Use oven mitts to remove the bowl and record from the oven and allow them to cool for a few minutes to solidify the shape.

WHISKEY-BOTTLE LIGHT

MATERIALS AND TOOLS

- EMPTY WHISKEY BOTTLE
- GLASS CUTTER
- GLOVES
- SAFETY GLASSES
- KITCHEN TOWEL OR OTHER CLOTH
- STEEL WOOL
- FINE-GRIT EMERY CLOTH
- SOLDERING IRON
- HEAT-SHRINK TUBING
- PENDANT LIGHT WITH CORD

Great whiskeys usually come in bottles with great label art or great shapes. Celebrate your good taste by making a bottle light that will provide some much-needed illumination in your otherwise-dark man cave. These pendant lamps can be draped over beams or easily hung from a ceiling with a wall hook. They're also a unique and fun way to show your whiskey allegiance.

1. You shouldn't have any trouble emptying the bottle. When you have, clean and dry it. With the bottom of the bottle on a flat surface, elevate the glass cutter so that the blade is about 1 inch from the bottom of the bottle. I found that the cork from my bottle held the glass cutter at the perfect height.

A glass cutter works by scoring a thin, shallow mark along the glass. Subsequent breakage is guided along this score. Round bottles work best for this dude craft, as it's easier to achieve a uniform score around a round circumference. However, with patience, this method can work on most bottle shapes. With the glass cutter in the right location, rotate the bottle to scribe a level line around its circumference. It's important, when cutting glass, to remember your safety gear, namely gloves and protective eyewear.

2. Place a cloth in the bottom of your sink to cushion the bottom of the bottle when it falls off. Run the scored area under hot water for about a minute, then change the temperature to cold. This sudden change will cause thermal stress in the glass and eventually create a fracture at the score line. Repeat the process of alternating hot and cold water to create a fracture around the score line until the bottle separates. Sometimes a light tap with the back end of the glass cutter can help things along.

3. Smooth over the cut edges with steel wool and then fine-grit emery cloth, taking time to ensure that all exposed edges are smoothed to prevent cut fingers.

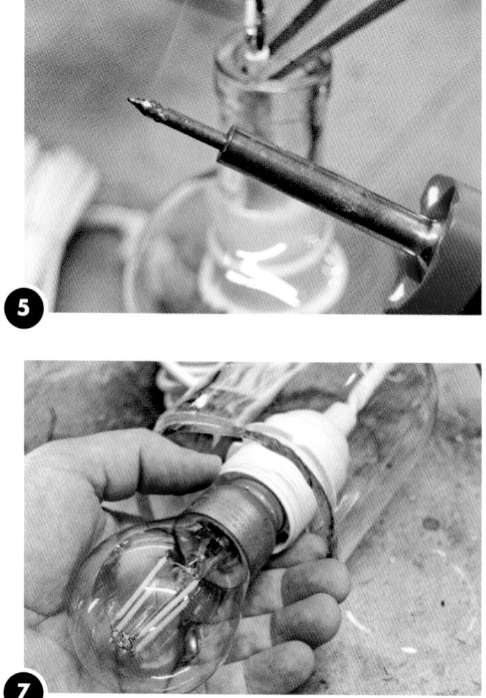

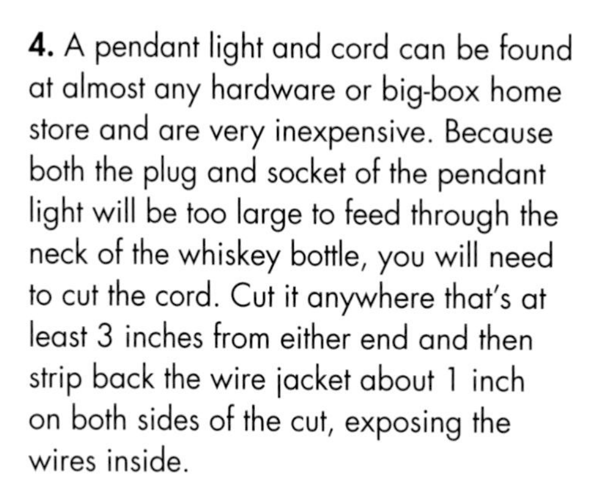

4. A pendant light and cord can be found at almost any hardware or big-box home store and are very inexpensive. Because both the plug and socket of the pendant light will be too large to feed through the neck of the whiskey bottle, you will need to cut the cord. Cut it anywhere that's at least 3 inches from either end and then strip back the wire jacket about 1 inch on both sides of the cut, exposing the wires inside.

5. Insert the socket side of the cut pendant light inside the bottle. Feed its wire through the neck opening and secure the socket inside the cut bottle. Slip a section of heat-shrink tubing over one of the cut ends and slide it about 2 inches past the cut end of the wire. Then solder the ends of the wire back together and use electrical tape to isolate the wires from each other.

6. Slide the heat-shrink over the exposed wires to cover them completely. Use heat radiating from the soldering iron to activate the heat-shrink and secure it over the exposed wires. Ideally, use a heat-shrink that matches the color of the cord.

7. To really make this lamp stand out, find a unique bulb to put inside. This vintage-looking bulb has a steampunk Edison vibe, complete with colored glass, but is actually an energy-efficient LED that doesn't produce as much heat as an incandescent bulb.

WINE-BOTTLE GLASS

MATERIALS AND TOOLS

- **GLASS CUTTER**
- **1-INCH SPACER**
- **GLOVES**
- **SAFETY GLASSES**
- **KITCHEN TOWEL OR OTHER CLOTH**
- **FINE-GRIT EMERY CLOTH**
- **STEEL WOOL**
- **E6000 ADHESIVE**

Curb your drinking habits by limiting yourself to one glass of wine a night. Luckily, this glass can hold an entire bottle—because it *is* a bottle!

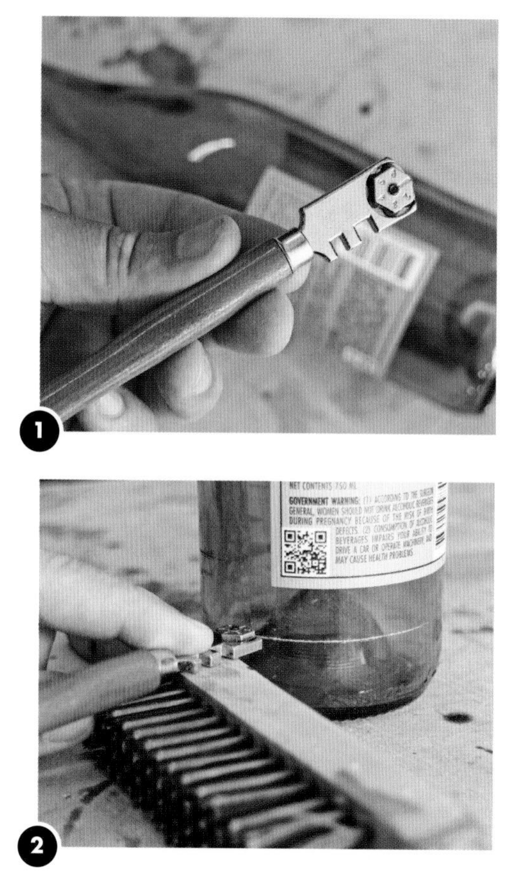

1. Glass cutters are inexpensive and make quick work of cutting through a wine bottle.

2. Stand the bottle upright and find a sturdy rectangular item about 1 inch tall, which you will use as a spacer. (I used the blocky handle of a wire brush I had in the shop.) Holding the glass cutter firmly on top of the spacer, push and rotate the wine bottle against the cutting head to create a level line around the entire circumference. The glass cutter will not cut all the way through the bottle; instead, it scores the glass and creates a fracture line where the bottle will split when stressed.

3. Place a cloth in the bottom of your sink to cushion the bottom of the bottle when it falls off. Run the scored area of the bottle under hot water for about twenty seconds, then immediately switch to cold water. Repeat this process a few times to shock the glass and cause a fracture that will separate the bottom of the bottle. In addition to laying down a cloth, it's a good idea to hold the bottle as close to the bottom of the sink as possible to avoid the glass shattering when the bottom falls out.

4

4. Once the bottom of the wine bottle has been separated from the top, gently rub the cut line with steel wool and then fine-grit emery cloth to create a smooth drinking edge. Take your time here; gloves and safety glasses are not a bad idea.

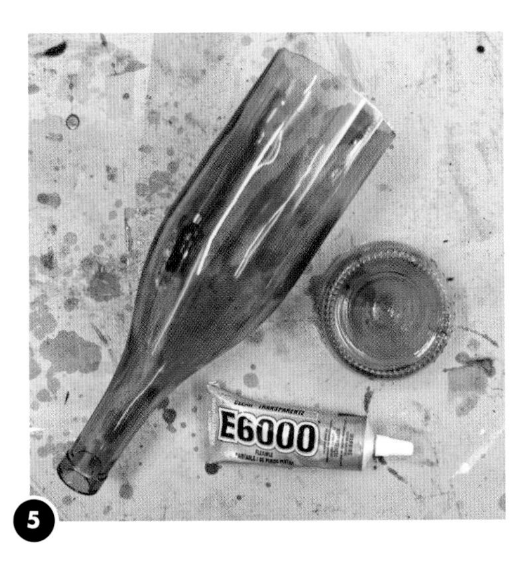

5

5. The last step is to attach the severed bottom of the bottle to the bottle neck to form the base. Use E6000, an industrial-strength adhesive that bonds glass. Apply a liberal amount to the mouth of the bottle, then adhere this glued end to the concave cavity on the upturned bottom of the wine bottle. The bottle will need to rest against something straight as the glue dries overnight to ensure the glass stands upright.

All that's left is to open a bottle of your favorite wine and pour yourself one—and only one—glass!

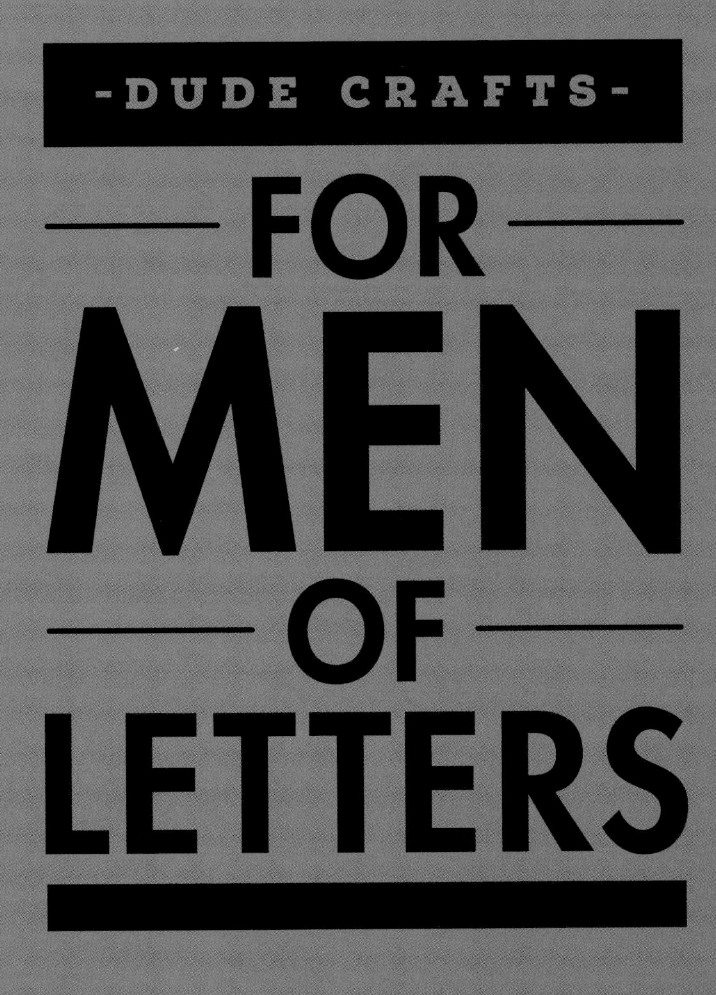
-DUDE CRAFTS-
FOR
MEN
OF
LETTERS

BOOK SAFE

MATERIALS AND TOOLS

- OLD HARDCOVER BOOK(S)
- PENCIL
- BANDSAW
- SCRAP ¼- TO ½-INCH PLYWOOD
- WOOD GLUE
- BAR CLAMP
- OFF-WHITE PAINT
- SCISSORS (OPTIONAL)
- HOBBY KNIFE (OPTIONAL)
- COTTON FABRIC (OPTIONAL)
- SPRAY ADHESIVE (OPTIONAL)

The book safe is a classic DIY project, but making one by tediously cutting out pages with an X-Acto knife is dangerous, difficult, and time consuming. Here's a faster and much easier solution that's flexible enough to allow book safes of just about any shape or size.

1. First, find a large hardcover book at a thrift store or yard sale (make sure it's one you don't want to read!) and sketch out the area you want to remove. Unlike cutting the opening with a knife, which requires a large border offset, using a bandsaw allows for a thin border and thus a much larger volume inside the book safe. Trace an outline on the first page of the book about ½ inch from the edges.

2. Fold back the front and back covers of the book and lay the pages flat on the bandsaw table. Slowly cut into each side of the pages (i.e., top and bottom of the pages) perpendicular to the spine. Cut a shallow radius when transitioning from one of these side cuts to the cut that runs parallel to the spine.

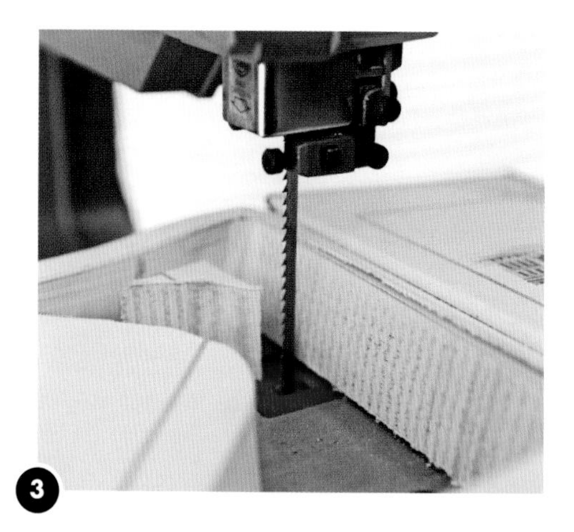

3. When you connect the two side cuts, remove the bulk of the pages, then turn the book around to resolve the leftover radius cut, thus creating two square corners.

4. If you like, you can find another similar-sized hardcover book and cut it in the same fashion to add onto your book safe. (If not, skip to step 5.) Here, I cut the second book using the first as a reference and made openings in the adjacent covers that will line up when the two books are glued together (the front cover of the bottom book and the back cover of the top one). This book safe will accommodate very large items.

5

5. This method removes most of the outside edges of the pages of the book, which is a giveaway if the book is off the shelf. Since these types of safes are rarely anywhere *but* on a bookshelf, this isn't an issue visually. However, the open side needs to be boxed up to contain the goodies inside. I cut a piece of scrap plywood to fit in the gap and used more wood glue to hold it in place. This piece of wood not only seals up the back of the book but holds the pages together and makes the entire safe more rigid. Clamp the book together with a bar clamp while the glue dries. After it's dry, paint the plywood an off-white color to deceive any quick glances.

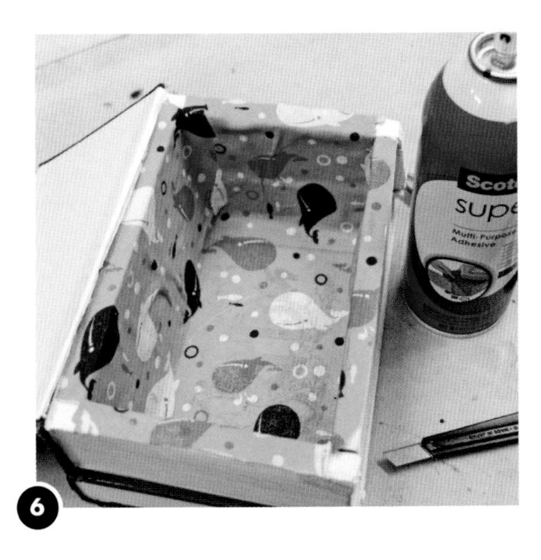

6

6. You can leave the safe as is, but I decided to line mine with fabric to "clean up" the inside. Simply use spray adhesive to bond the fabric to the inside of the book safe, then trim the edges for a neat and more finished look.

DINOSAUR PENCIL SHARPENER

MATERIALS AND TOOLS

- **PLASTIC TOY DINOSAUR**
- **PENCIL SHARPENER**
- **DRILL AND BITS**
- **POCKETKNIFE**
- **TWO-PART EPOXY**

In my workshop, just about every idea I have starts as a pencil sketch. I sometimes use a knife to whittle away the ends of dull pencils to sharpen them, but that's nowhere near as fun as using good ol' T-rex to sharpen my idea sketcher.

In fact, I keep a few toys around my shop for inspiration and to relax my mind when some projects get tough and I need a break. It might seem silly, but sometimes mindless distraction is just what's needed to free up a mental logjam—and if I can combine these toys with a functional element, they are even more valuable to my shop!

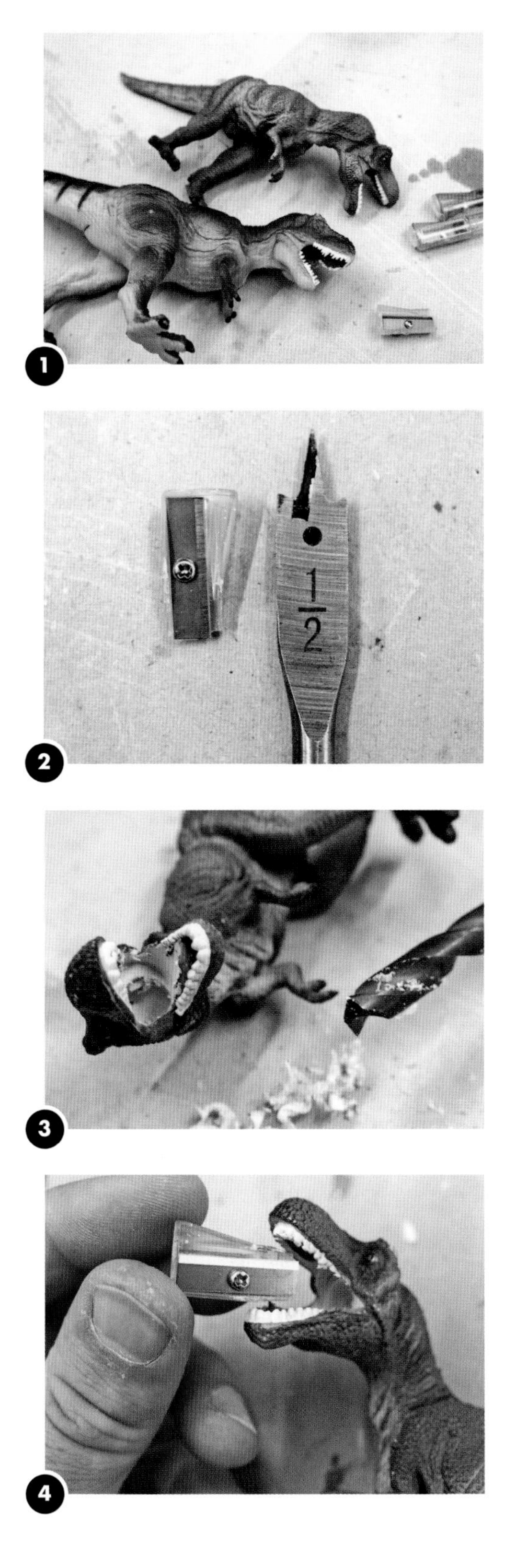

1. These dinosaurs have large, roaring mouths, and pencil sharpeners seem like appropriate fits for those sharp teeth. How much oral surgery you need to perform on your dinosaur depends on the sharpener and the dino itself, but you'll want to at least start with an open-mouthed toy.

2. I used a spade bit around the same size as my pencil sharpener to make an opening in the dinosaur's mouth to create a cavity where I could install the sharpener. I had to use my pocketknife to whittle away some material from the plastic sharpener housing to make it fit snugly.

3. Next, I used a second, smaller drill bit to create a cavity behind the main opening to accommodate the taper at the back of the sharpener.

4. Whatever plastic animal you choose to house your pencil sharpener, allow room for the pencil shavings to fall freely from the sharpener. Any obstruction can cause the sharpener to jam and not work—and removing pencil shavings from a hard-to-reach place is not fun.

Mix a strong two-part epoxy and use it to secure the pencil sharpener into the dinosaur mouth. Allow the epoxy a full day to cure before using. Now your brain-break toy has double duty as your idea-stick sharpener!

INVISIBLE BOOKSHELF

MATERIALS AND TOOLS

- OLD HARDCOVER BOOK
- TWO STEEL L-BRACKETS
- PENCIL
- HOBBY KNIFE
- CLAMPS
- DRILL AND DRIVER BIT
- WOOD SCREWS
- WALL-MOUNTING SCREWS WITH APPROPRIATE ANCHORS

A shelf that makes it look your books are suspended on your wall by pure magic! This clever trick allows you to mount a shelf within a hardcover book, obscuring the mounting hardware. This simple hack is a great way to display your books and show off your crafty DIY knowledge.

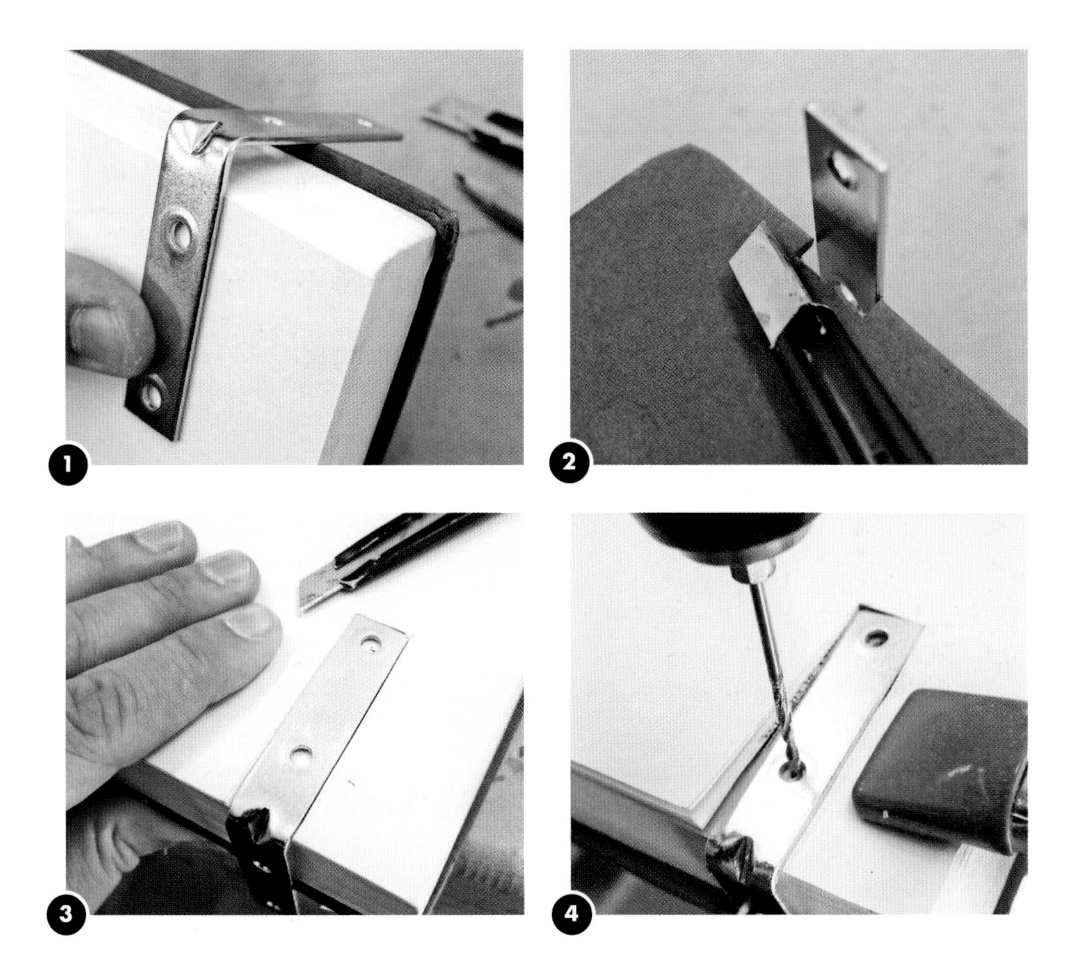

1. Open to the back of the hardcover book and place an L-bracket so it's seated 1 to 2 inches from the top edge of the page with the L's long edge extending toward the front cover. With a pencil, sketch the outline of the L-bracket on the last page and the edge of the front cover.

2. Use a sharp hobby knife to remove the notch from the edge of the front cover, allowing the L-bracket's upright to sit flush against the edges of the pages.

3. Replace the L-bracket and use the hobby knife to cut enough pages from the outline traced on the last page to allow the L-bracket to sit flush with the top of the last page.

4. Pencil in the L-bracket's drill holes on the page and use a drill to make small pilot holes at the marks.

5

5. With the book clamped tightly, attach screws through the L-bracket and into the drilled openings. This will secure the book closed and affix the bracket to the book. You must have the book clamped tightly before inserting the screws or the pages will separate as the screws are inserted, puffing up the pages.

Repeat this entire process with the second L-bracket near the bottom edge of the page.

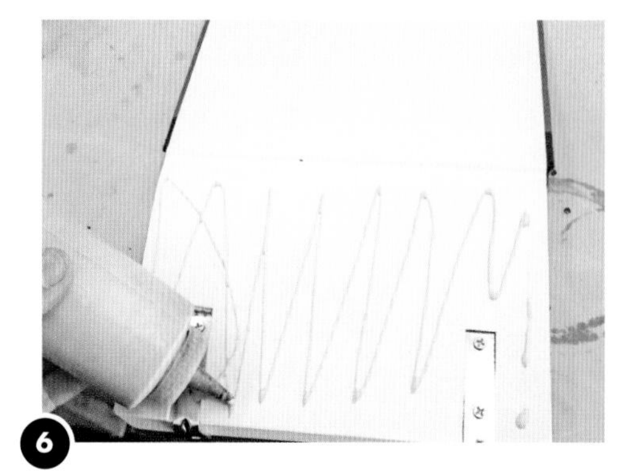

6

6. With both brackets installed, glue the back cover closed over the bracket to hide the mounting hardware.

7

7. To mount, locate a stud in your wall and screw one L-bracket into the stud to bear any type of weight. The other L-bracket can be drilled into a wall anchor. Then, pile a few books on your invisible bookshelf and amaze your friends!

TABLET BOOK COVER

MATERIALS AND TOOLS

- OLD HARDCOVER BOOK WITH GLUED BINDING
- TABLET OR E-READER
- HOBBY KNIFE
- FABRIC ELASTIC
- DRILL AND FOUR SCREWS
- WHITE CRAFT GLUE

Sure, you can choose from thousands of covers to protect your personal tablet, but those store-bought ones are all fairly boring. Why not make a cover that really speaks to who you are by using an old hardcover copy of your favorite book? Just like those store-bought versions, this cover will protect your tablet from bumps and scratches while not-so-subtly advertising your inner nerd (Jules Verne or Isaac Asimov, anyone?) *and* concealing your tablet inside an unexpected item.

1. First, find a hardcover book that's slightly larger than your tablet. You can easily find one on the cheap at a thrift store, yard sale, or library sale. It's important that the book have a glued rather than sewn binding. The easiest way to tell if it's *not* sewn is to examine the gutter between opened pages, where a sewn binding will reveal stitches if you open it far enough.

2. Use a sharp hobby knife to cut the book's binding and release the pages from the front cover.

3. Next, working from the glued edge of the pages, cut from the top a thickness of pages that matches the thickness of your tablet. Place the tablet inside and check the fit; your book should be able to shut completely with forcing it.

4. Now drill four small holes, one near each corner of the exposed pages. These holes are where screws will hold the elastic in place and keep the pages fastened shut. To hold the pages in place, you can either glue the pages together using a clamp with a flat piece of wood and allow it to dry, or you can use longer screws to bite into the back cover and trim them flush with a rotary cutter.

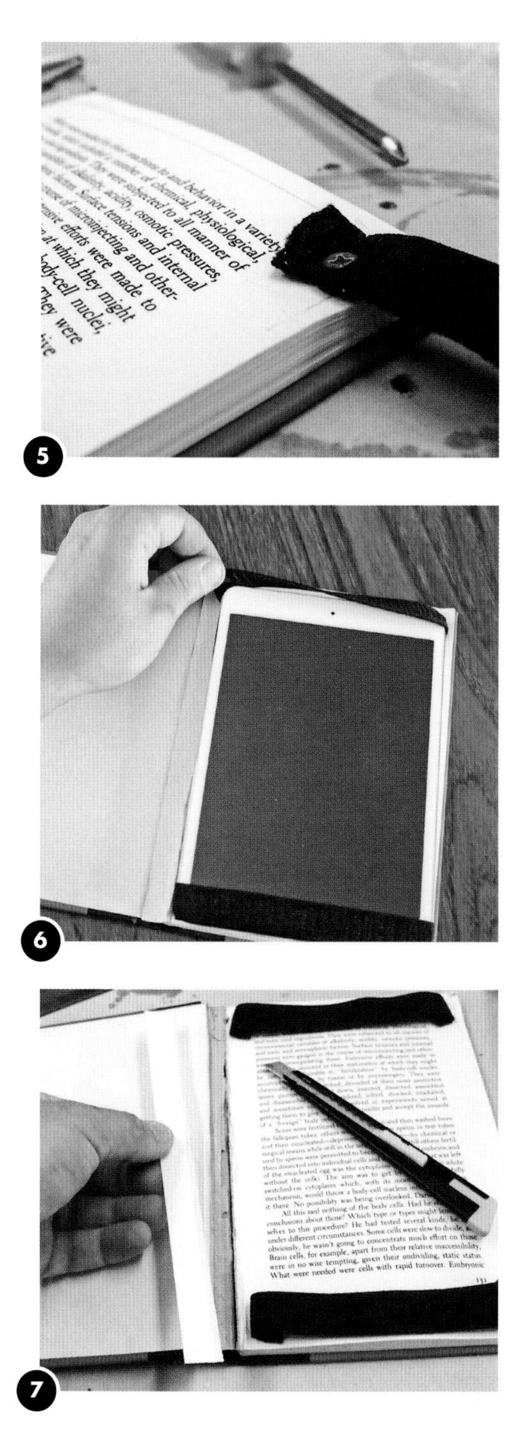

5. Cut two lengths of the fabric elastic, each about 2 inches longer than the width of your tablet. Use tapered-head screws to secure the fabric to the book using the holes drilled earlier. Secure one end of the fabric elastic to the book with the end of the elastic facing inward toward the center of the page. Tapered-head screws will sink into the elastic and act as a countersink, preventing the head from scratching your tablet. Fold the elastic over, placing the free end inward so it mirrors the other side, then secure with another screw.

6. Repeat the process with the elastic and screws using the two holes at the bottom of the page. The top and the bottom elastics should match, and the elastic should be short enough to secure the tablet when placed inside.

7. Scrape any excess dried binding glue from the exposed inside of the spine and then glue in a scrap of paper cut to width from the excess pages you cut from the book. This gives a nice clean finish to the book.

-DUDE CRAFTS-
HIGH-
BROW
COMEDY

CAR-EXHAUST HORN

MATERIALS AND TOOLS

- CALIPERS OR TAPE MEASURE
- PEN
- HIGH-TEMPERATURE GASKET MAKER
- HOBBY KNIFE
- ROUND SOLID PLASTIC TO FIT TAILPIPE
- DRILL AND BIT ABOUT THE SAME SIZE AS YOUR NOISEMAKER
- PARTY NOISEMAKERS
- E6000 ADHESIVE
- HOT-GLUE GUN

This modern update to the classic banana-in-the-tailpipe prank uses party kazoos to make a loud noise when the car is revved. A solid plastic block plugs the exhaust, while sized openings for kazoos force the exhaust through the noise maker. A high-heat gasket protects the plastic from direct contact with the hot tailpipe, allowing this gag to be used multiple times without any damage to the car or prank device.

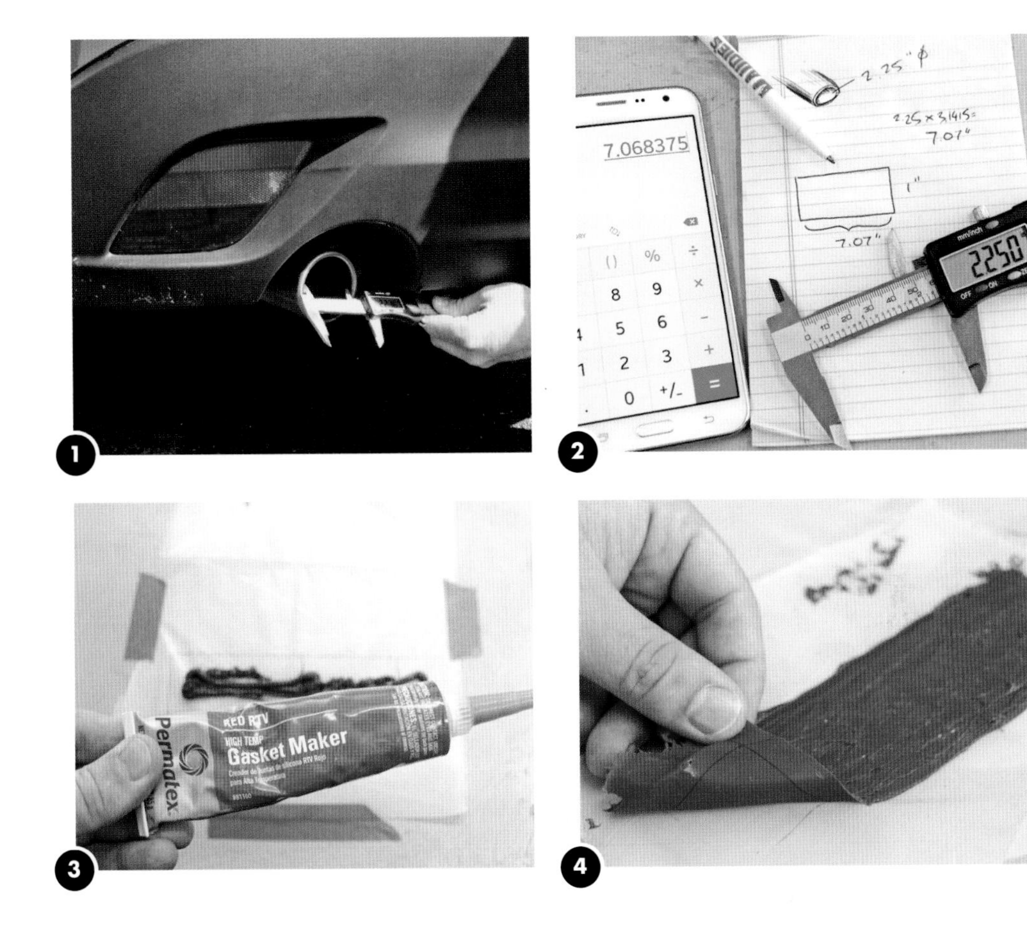

1. Use calipers to measure the interior diameter (*d*) of the target tailpipe.

2. Using some simple math ($C=\pi d$), determine the circumference (C) of the tailpipe. This is the length of the gasket needed to sit inside the tailpipe and prevent the noisemaker holder and noisemakers from melting.

3. I used high-temp liquid gasket maker to get the shape I needed, but any high-heat gasket material will work. Sketch out the size of the gasket needed on a scrap piece of plastic.

4. Spread a thick layer of the liquid gasket just outside the sketch marks, ensuring the gasket will be large enough. After letting the gasket cure overnight, it will easily peel off the plastic. The pen sketch marks should transfer onto the underside of the gasket, leaving a clear guide for trimming with your hobby knife.

4. I made this noisemaker holder from a 3D-printed piece of plastic, but any piece of plastic cut to size will work. It just needs to be large enough to fit inside the tailpipe and sturdy enough to hold the noisemakers. Drill holes in the plastic sized to accept the noisemaker mouthpieces snugly, then glue the trimmed gasket around the circumference of the plastic block using E6000 adhesive. After allowing it to cure overnight, the piece is ready to be installed.

5. Secure the party noisemakers in place with small dabs of hot glue around the edges. Make sure not to cover the holes of the noisemakers with glue.

6. The last step is to secretly place the prank into the tailpipe of your target while they are unaware. The noise starts when the driver gets up to speed. Chances are he or she won't be aware it's their car making the noise for some time, allowing onlookers and passengers a good laugh at their expense.

FIRE BREATHER

MATERIALS AND TOOLS

- CORNSTARCH
- EMPTY 6- OR 8-OUNCE PLASTIC WATER BOTTLE (OPTIONAL)
- PROPANE TORCH OR LIGHTER

Channel your inner carnival performer by breathing fire! This easy party pyrotechnic can be done with a lots of different starch powders, like cornstarch and potato starch—it even works with nondairy powdered creamer.

1. The quick, easy, and safer way to perform this trick is to fill a small, dry plastic water bottle about one-quarter full of cornstarch.

2. Poke a small hole in the cap and screw it onto the bottle.

3. Holding the bottle sideways, squeeze it with the cap pointing toward the flame source, like a lighted propane torch. The air pressure created by squeezing the bottle will push air and cornstarch out of the lid opening, aerosolizing the cornstarch. The mist-like powder will ignite and create a large fireball.

A more dramatic presentation is to put a heaping spoonful of cornstarch in your mouth, then blow it out using your pursed lips to create an aerosolized cloud of starch easily ignited by a flame from a lighter. The technique involved in blowing the starch and determining the correct distance from the flame takes some refinement, but once you get it right, you'll be the hit of the party. The fireball dissipates quickly and you're ready to blow another. Just make sure you have a tall glass of water on hand, as cornstarch will make your mouth funky afterward. Be careful (and have fun).

HEAD IN A JAR

MATERIALS AND TOOLS

- DIGITAL CAMERA
- COMPUTER PAPER AND PRINTER
- SCISSORS OR HOBBY KNIFE
- CLEAR TAPE
- PAPER LAMINATOR
- LARGE GLASS JAR
- FOOD COLORING
- OLD WIG (OPTIONAL)

Inexpensive and incredibly effective, this one is guaranteed results every April Fools' or Halloween. Whether it's your head or your friend's stuck inside the jar, shrieks, laughs, and perhaps even involuntary bladder movements are sure to ensue with this perennial classic.

1. Start by taking one head-on and one profile shot of your subject. You can easily mirror the profile picture in almost any photo-editing software to create the other side of the head. If you're savvy with photo-editing software, you can blend the three images together to create a single image to print. Photo-editing software is available online for free. Alternatively, simply print out the head-on picture and both sides of the profile on a color printer, ensuring the head completely fills the pages.

2. Use scissors or a sharp hobby knife to trim away any white borders from the printouts. If you didn't blend the three images together with editing software, cut the profile images vertically at the eyes and match each side to the head-on image. Use clear tape to secure the images together.

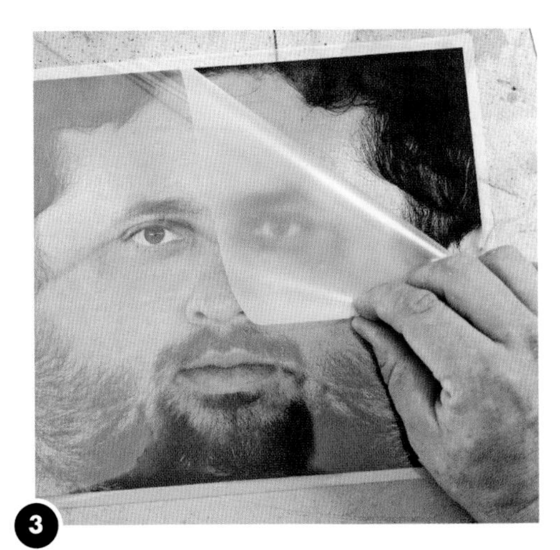

3

3. Use an office lamination machine to completely encase the image in a protective plastic casing. If you don't have access to an office laminator, big-box office supply stores offer this service. Once the picture is laminated, turn your attention to the jar.

4

4. Find a clear glass jar large enough to hold the laminated picture and fill it with water, leaving about an inch of room at the top. Add a few drops of red and green food coloring to give the water a murky, formaldehyde-like appearance.

5

5. Curl the laminated image and insert into the jar, ensuring the face is pressed against the glass. A wig in a color similar to the subject's own hair helps to sell the illusion and takes this project from "meh" to "mehhhhOHMYGODWHATISTHAT?!" Place the wig over the top edge of the laminated picture. This also helps hide the top edge of the lamination.

6

6. Put the lid on the jar and place it somewhere inconspicuous, like the fridge. Then, just lurk and wait for the victim to happen upon it!

OFFICE-CHAIR AIR HORN

MATERIALS AND TOOLS

- SMALL AIR HORN
- BLACK ELECTRICAL TAPE
- ZIP TIES (BLACK, IF POSSIBLE)
- SCISSORS

Few things satisfy like a good office prank. This simple gag deploys an air horn under your colleague's office chair and uses the victim's own body weight to trigger the horn.

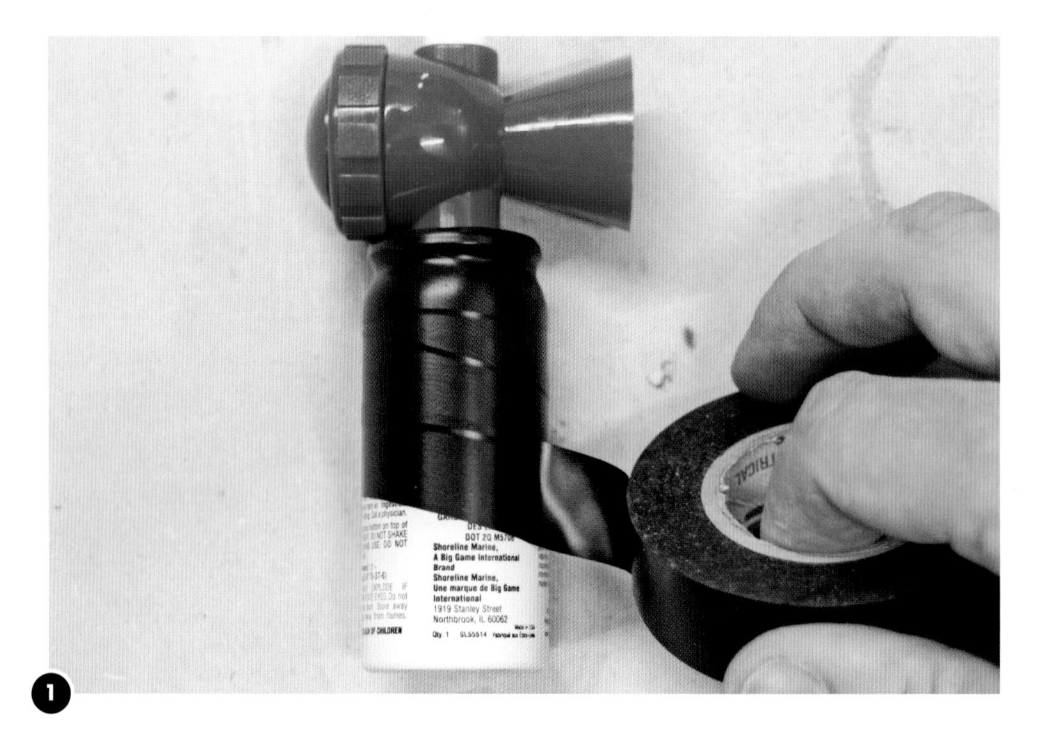

1

2

1. Wrap your air horn in black electrical tape to help camouflage it, since the colorful body of the can could attract attention and foil the prank.

2. Most adjustable chairs have a ledge on the piston that controls the seat height. Place the air horn on this ledge and zip-tie the body of the air horn loosely to the chair piston.

3. Position the top of the horn just below the lowest part of the seat, ensuring trigger contact when the victim sits in the chair. Then, tighten the zip ties and clip the tails to clean up the appearance. You can see I used black here as well to help conceal the ties.

Now be cool and walk away like nothing happened—but stay close by to enjoy the look of terror when your coworker sits down to another day of drudgery only to be greeted by a sharp blast of the air horn, made all the sweeter because it was triggered by their own actions!

OFFICE-SUPPLY CROSSBOW

MATERIALS AND TOOLS

- FOUR PENCILS
- ONE BALLPOINT PEN
- TWELVE RUBBER BANDS
- ONE BINDER CLIP
- MASKING TAPE

Cubicle warfare can be a serious affair. The next time your cubicle neighbor takes your stapler or socializes loudly while you're trying to work, bring the war to their doorstep. This pen-and-pencil shooter is perfect for having some harmless fun and flexing your engineering muscles.

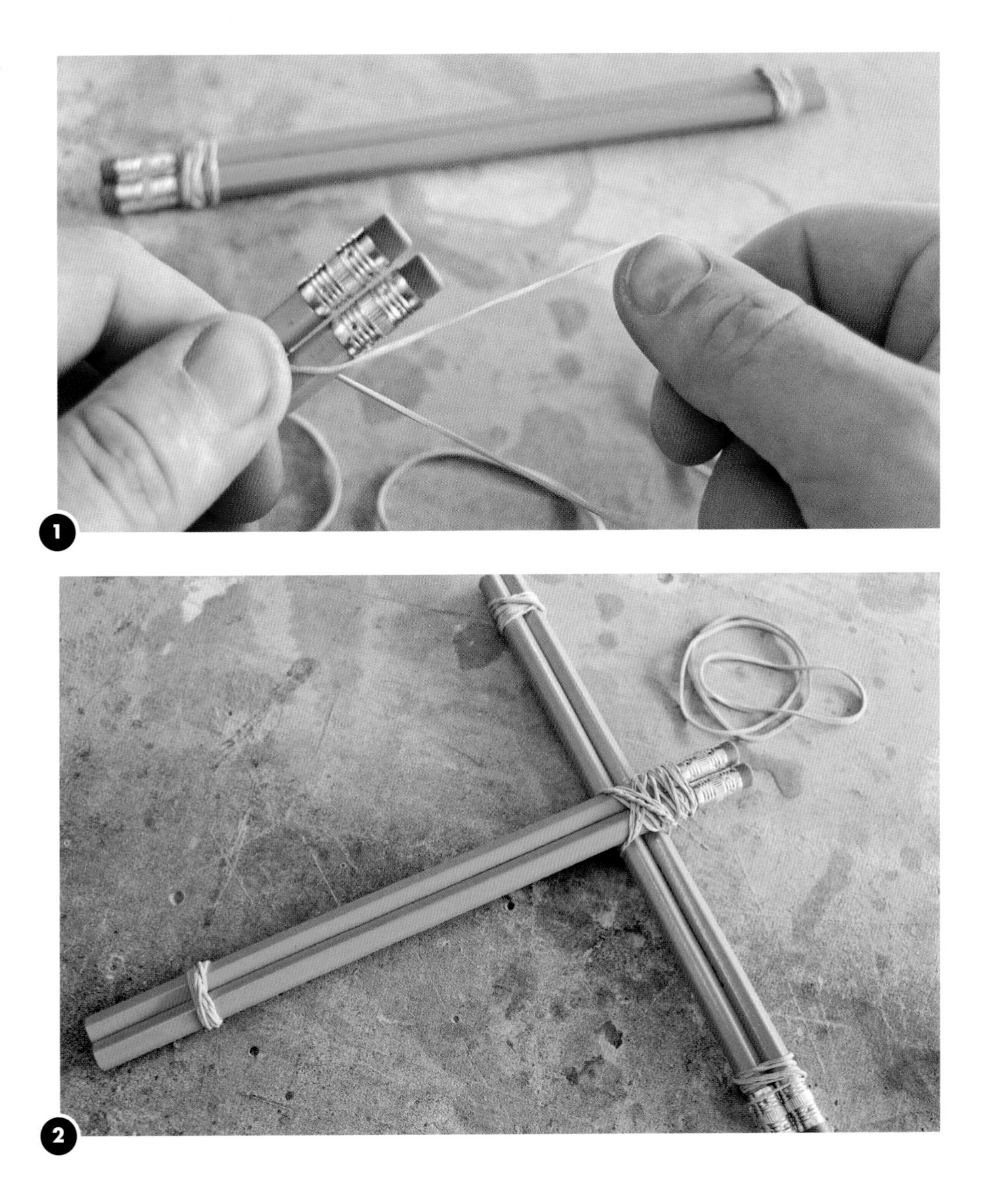

1. The basics are easy enough to learn, but there are endless ways to modify this design to make it your own. Start by combining two pairs of pencils, securing them together with a rubber band at each end.

2. Use two more rubber bands to secure the two pencil sets perpendicular to each other, forming a T shape. You now have the chassis for your crossbow.

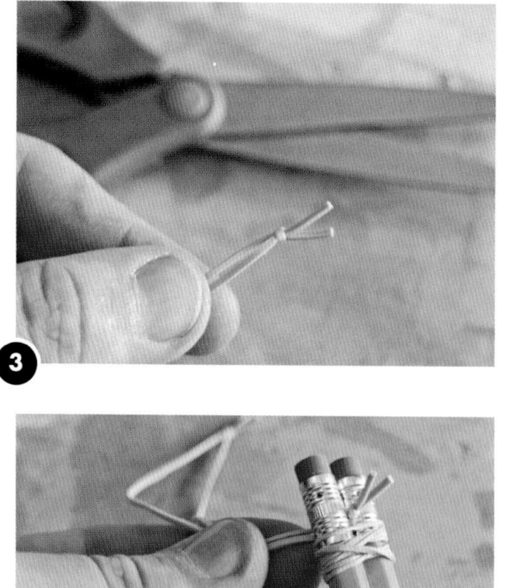

3. Next, snip two rubber bands, lay them side by side, and tie the ends together to make a double rubber-band strip. Make sure the knots are as close to the ends of the cut bands as possible.

4. Secure the knotted ends between the pencils at both ends of the crossbow-chassis crosspiece (i.e., the top of the T shape).

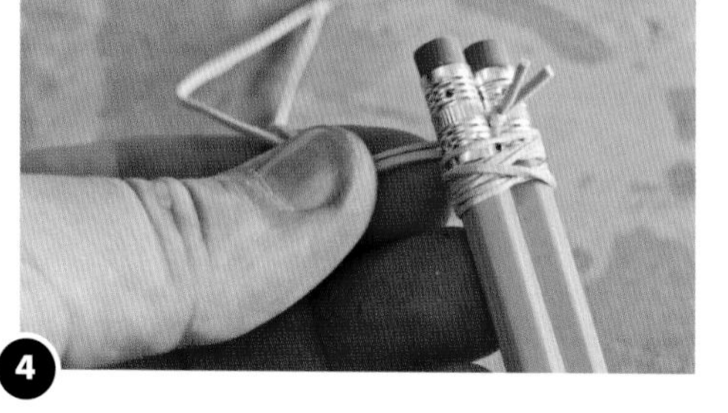

5. Remove the pen's innards so all that is left is the outer shell. The pen housing serves as the barrel, and the ink tube is the projectile. Use more rubber bands to secure the housing to the length of the crossbow chassis (i.e., the stem of the T shape), making sure one end crosses over the intersection of the T shape. This will help ensure maximum accuracy.

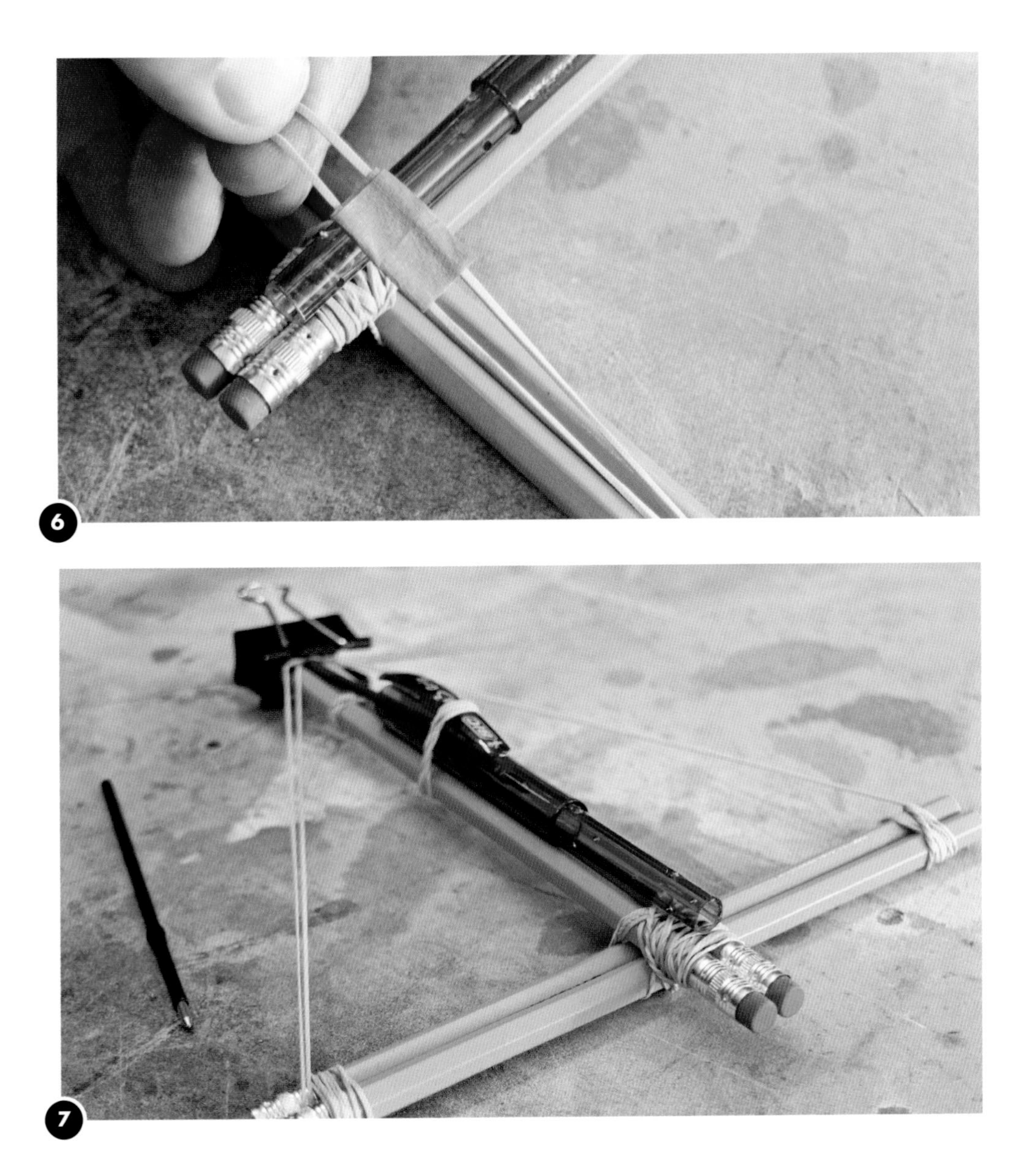

6. The cut rubber bands will launch the projectile through the pen housing. A small piece of masking tape wrapped around the midpoint of the cut rubber bands serves as a pouch to help hold the projectile in place before it's fired.

7. A binder clip attached to the end of the crossbow chassis holds the rubber bands taut when drawn back. Insert the pen-tube projectile into the pen housing and place the end of the tube in the masking-tape pouch. Draw the cartridge and rubber bands back and secure in place with the binder clip. Simply press the binder clip open to release the projectile.

Meant more as a nuisance than a real threat, this office supply armament can be modified in endless ways. To be safe, just keep the shots below the neck.

RAINY-DAY GRAFFITI

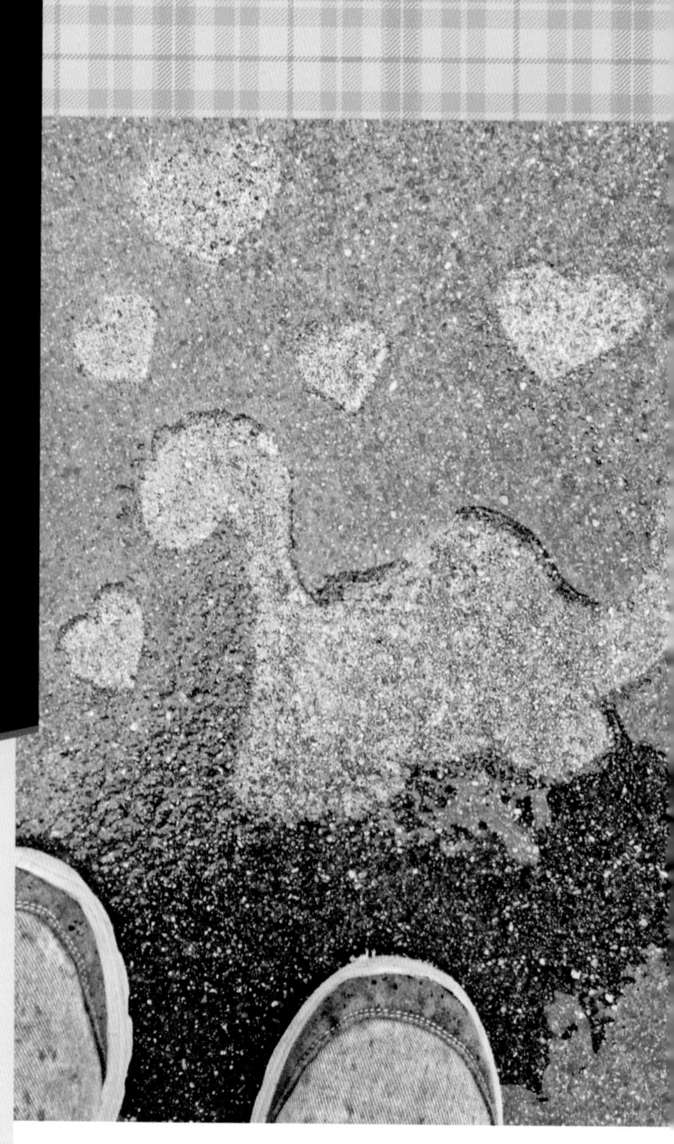

MATERIALS AND TOOLS

- CARDBOARD
- MARKER
- SHARP KNIFE
- CLEAR WATER-REPELLENT SPRAY

Is it still vandalism if there's no evidence? Spray this graffiti wherever you like—it appears only when it rains. A water-repellent clear spray, such as Rust-Oleum NeverWet, repels water from a surface as the areas around it absorb water. The effect is the painted area remains its natural lighter color while the areas around it darken with moisture. Though typically used for items you want to keep dry, there's no reason you can't make your statement by using this spray on the sidewalk.

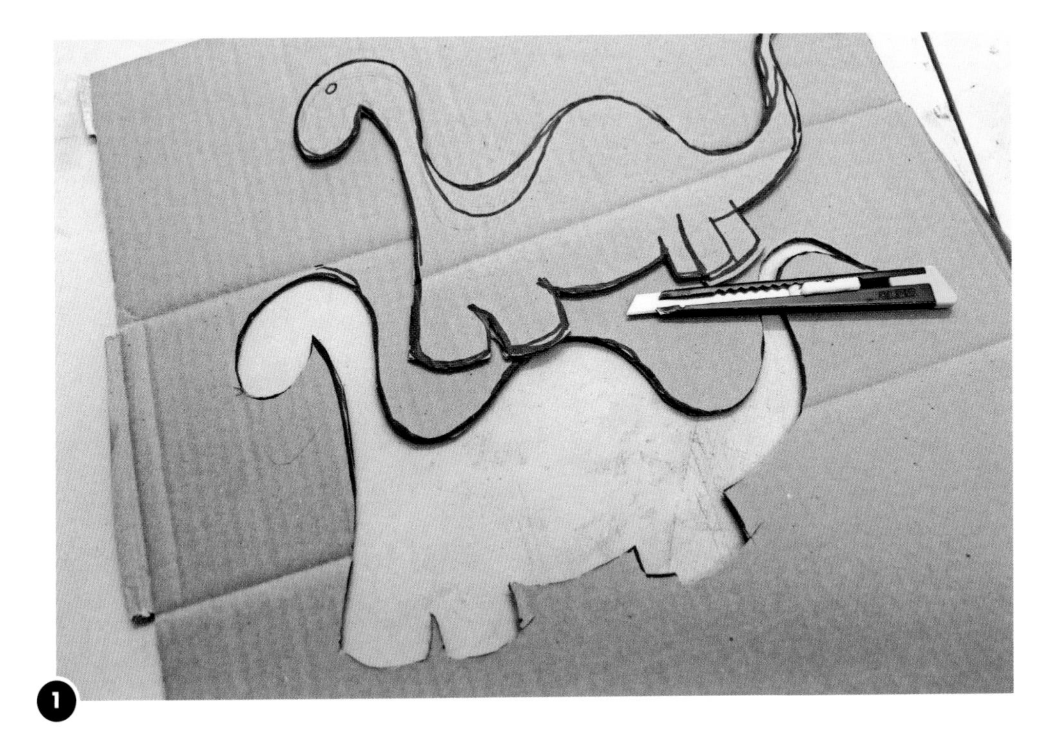

1. Because the spray is clear, you can't see it upon application. Also, you'll need to make multiple passes for best coverage, so it's ideal to use a stencil to control the area of your image. Sketch out patterns, shapes, or letters on cardboard and then cut them out using a sharp knife. Crisp edges are best as they leave the most defined shape.

2. The type of spray you use will determine how many coats you need to apply. At the least, you'll want multiple layers to achieve a strong and lasting effect.

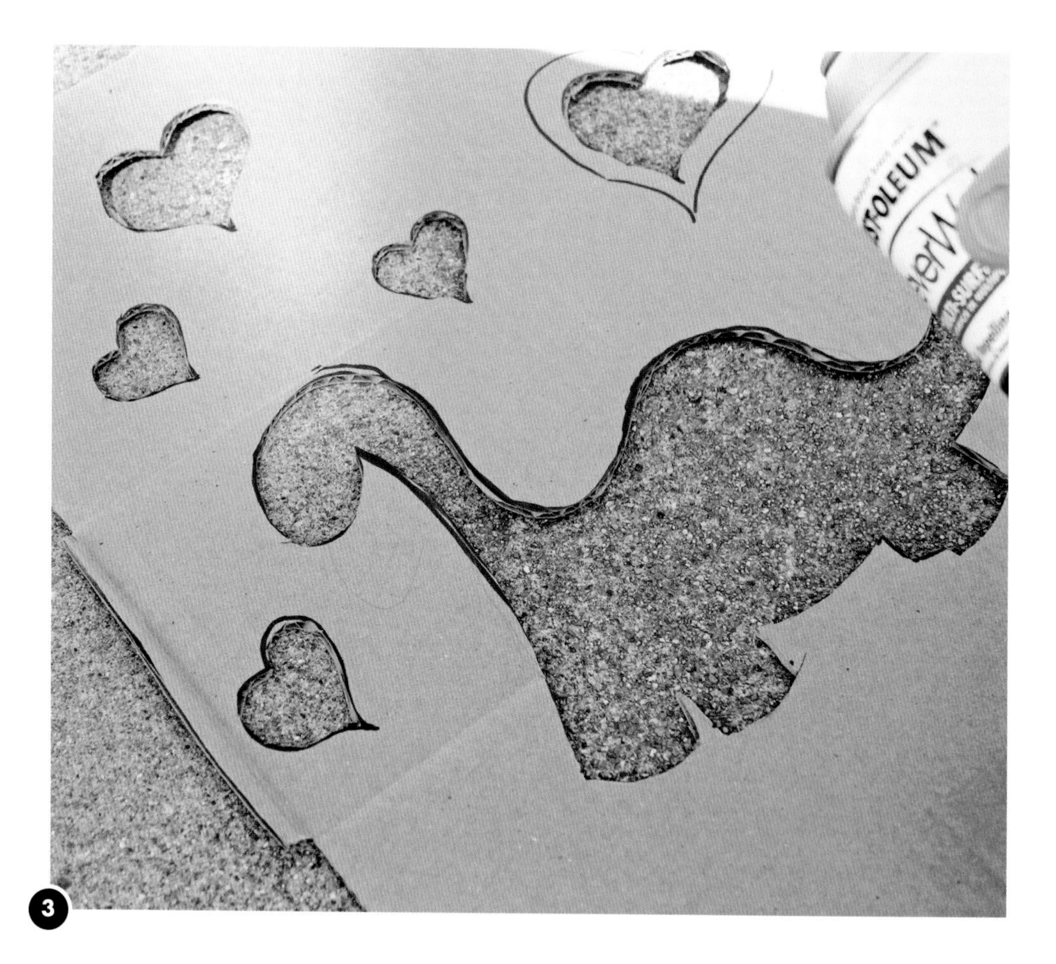

3

Place your stencil on the sidewalk where you want your graffiti, then hold it in place with rocks so it doesn't move during application. Spray your hydrophobic solution, making sure to spray perpendicular to the stencil so the spray doesn't work its way under the stencil edges. Overspray will ruin the sharp lines. Wait for the application to dry completely before applying the second coat. Remove the stencil and wait for the next rainstorm to reveal your waterproof graffiti.

SPILLED COFFEE

MATERIALS AND TOOLS

- OLD COFFEE MUG
- CLEAR TWO-PART EPOXY
- PAINT (BROWN AND WHITE)
- CRAFT STICK
- PARCHMENT OR WAX PAPER

Few office occurrences are more maddening than an accidentally spilled cup of coffee—maybe more so for the loss of a good beverage than the mess it creates (or the damage it causes). You can induce the stomach-dropping fear that comes when a cup of spilled coffee damages someone's laptop or important documents, all without causing any real damage.

Be warned that this prank will render a cup unusable for future beverages. While it's not advisable to use your boss's favorite cup, a cup that is known to the victim will be more compelling than a random mug from the local thrift store. Most offices have a collection of communal coffee cups—see if you can find an old one that no one will miss.

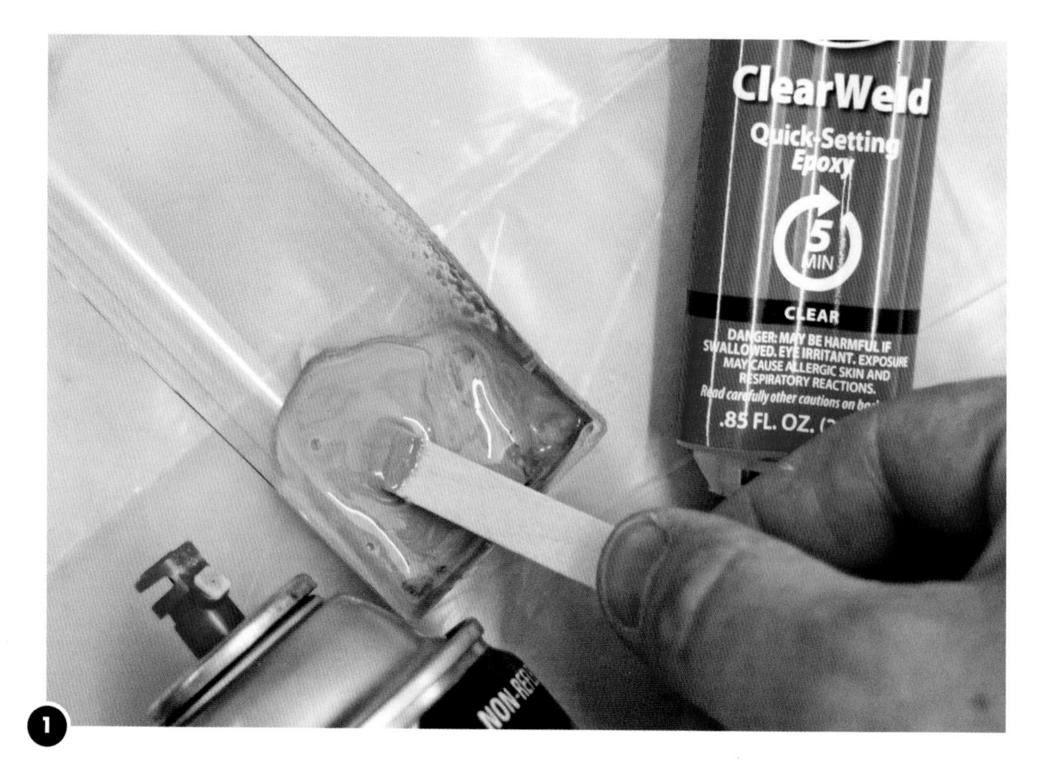

1

2

1. Start out by squirting 2 to 3 ounces of epoxy into a plastic container and mixing until combined. Add in a small amount of any latex or spray paint to achieve the right color for the drink. I used a light brown spray paint, though brown latex paint mixed with a small amount of white will also render the right shade simulating coffee with cream. Either way, mix the paint into the epoxy until you achieve a consistent color.

2. Place a sheet of parchment or wax paper on your work surface to protect the area. Lay the mug sideways on the paper and carefully pour the epoxy/paint mixture into the mug near the rim, dribbling a trail outside the mug to form a puddle.

3

3. Epoxy takes a few minutes to set, so you have a little time to make minor adjustments with your craft stick. Move the epoxy around to get a shape that best resembles a puddle that freshly spilled coffee might make. Leave the epoxy to cure overnight before handling.

4

4. Once it's cured, lift the mug and parchment or wax paper as one and stand the mug upright. Carefully peel away the parchment to reveal the prank mug. This is important: if you try to peel the cured epoxy off the paper from its horizontal position, you'll be more likely to break your epoxy "puddle."

All that's left is to place your mug on your victim's computer or paperwork—and hide nearby to witness their reaction!

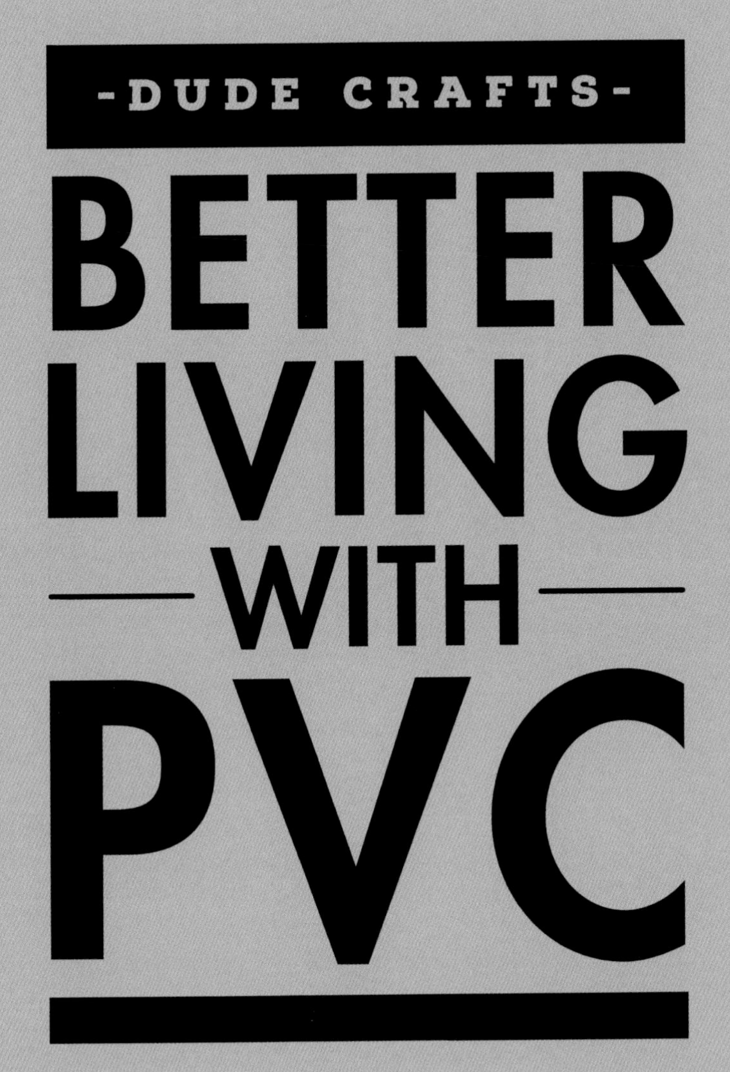
-DUDE CRAFTS-
BETTER
LIVING
WITH
PVC

AIR HORN

MATERIALS AND TOOLS

- 7-INCH LENGTH OF 1-INCH PVC PIPE
- 2-TO-1-INCH PVC TEE-REDUCER WITH THREADED 1-INCH OUTLET
- 2-INCH PVC REDUCER BUSHING
- 1-INCH PVC THREADED PLUG
- OLD BICYCLE INNER TUBE
- DRILL AND BIT
- ZIP TIE
- COMPRESSOR OR BIKE PUMP

This simple project uses a few pieces of PVC and an old bicycle inner tube as a diaphragm to create a very loud air horn. How this air horn works is deceptively simple: The inner pipe is held in place by the larger pipe and the reducer bushing, and the end of the inner pipe is pushed against the inner-tube diaphragm. When air is pumped into the larger sealed chamber, it forces the diaphragm to expand, releasing air out of the back (non-diaphragm end) of the inner pipe. Once the pressure is relieved, the diaphragm snaps shut against the inner pipe, sealing the air inside and making a sound when the diaphragm closes. This happens many times a second to create a loud, horn-like sound as air is continuously pumped into the cavity.

It might sound complicated, but it's very simple when you see it in action. And once you build it, you can modify it to make all kinds of sounds!

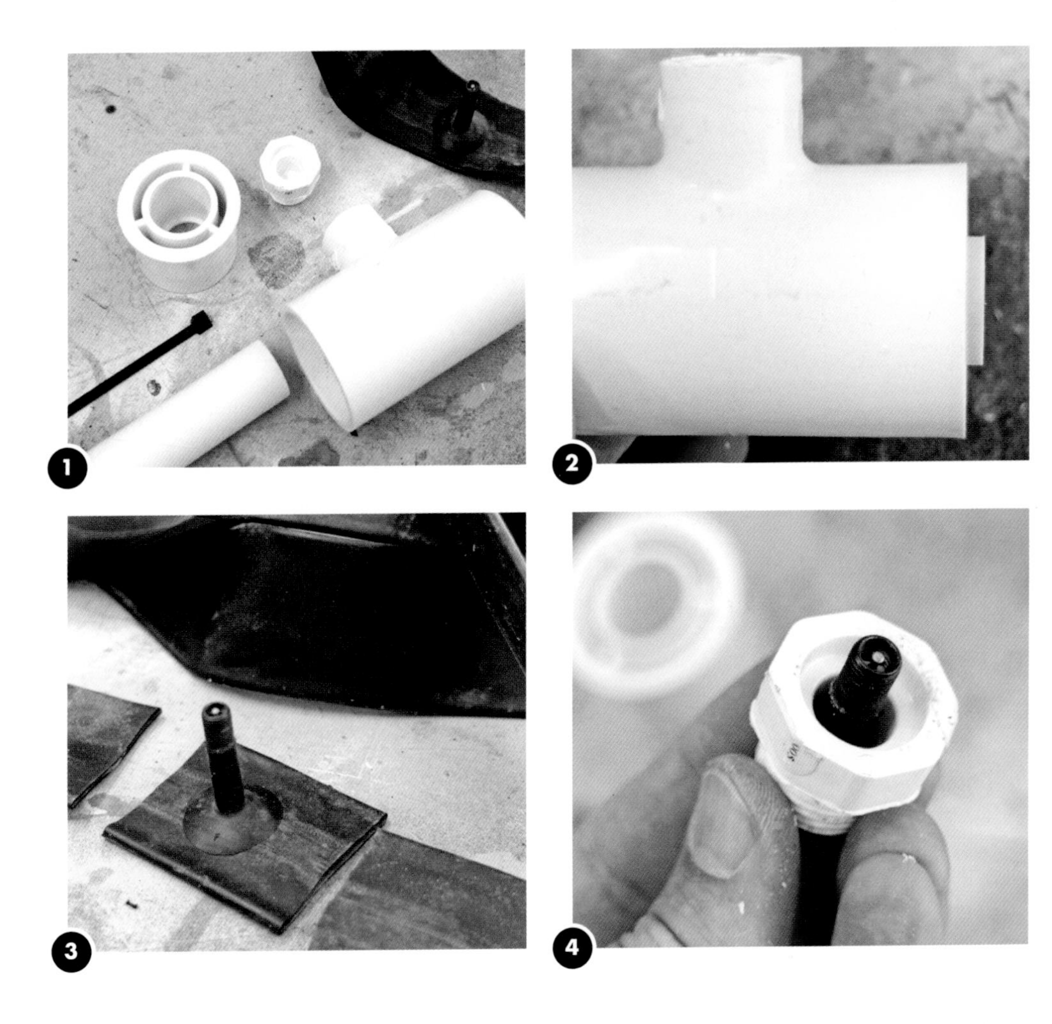

1. Start by inserting the 1-inch PVC pipe into the tee reducer. Some tee reducers have a small lip on the inside that prevents the pipe from slipping too far inside; if this is the case, sand the lip so the 1-inch pipe slides easily into the reducer. Insert the reducer bushing into one end of the tee and insert the 1-inch pipe into the bushing.

2. The 1-inch inner pipe should stick out from the other end of the tee just a touch.

3. Cut the valve stem from the inner tube, leaving a skirt of rubber at its base.

4. The tee reducer has a threaded opening in its 1-inch outlet, so I used this threaded plug to hold the valve stem in place, securing the stem's rubber skirt between the threads. I simply drilled a hole in the plug through which to insert the stem.

5. Cut out a small circle of the bike inner tube about 3 to 4 inches in diameter and lay it flat. Stretch this diaphragm over the open end of the tee reducer and secure it with a zip tie. Be sure to pull the diaphragm tight as you cinch it with a zip tie.

6. The 1-inch PVC pipe should be visibly pressing against the inner tube. If not, gently push the 1-inch pipe from the other end until it is pushing against the diaphragm. The tighter the inner tube is against the 1-inch pipe, the louder the noise will be.

7. Attach your compressor or bike pump to the inner tube stem and push air into the unit to build pressure. When the pressure is enough to move the diaphragm, the air horn will sound.

This project does not use any PVC glue, so all the parts can be disassembled or modified to create new sounds. A longer 1-inch pipe, for example, will create a deeper sound, and a tighter diaphragm will make the noise louder!

BALLOON SLINGSHOT

MATERIALS AND TOOLS

- 1-INCH LENGTH OF 1- OR 1½-INCH PVC PIPE
- SANDPAPER
- SCISSORS
- BALLOON
- ZIP TIE (OPTIONAL)

There's beauty in simplicity, and this stealthy slingshot-type shooter is as simple as it gets.

1

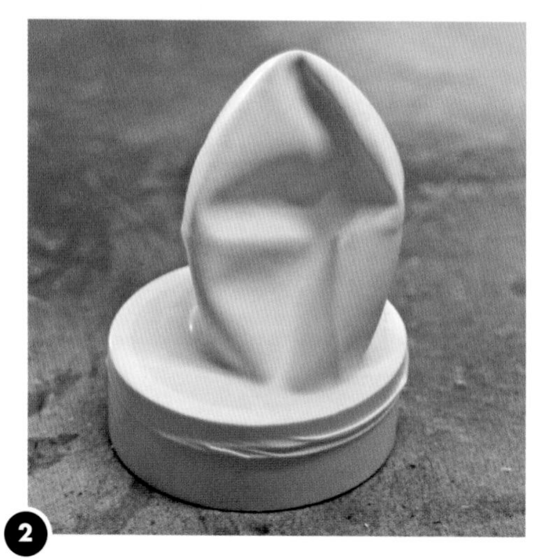

2

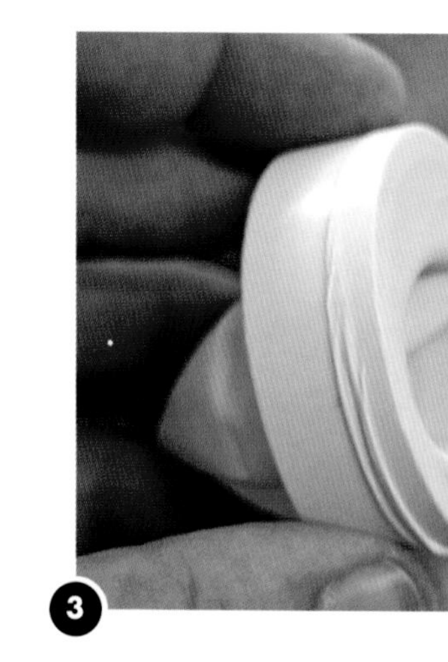

3

1. Cut a short section of PVC pipe and sand each end of the PVC pipe to remove any sharp burrs.

2. Cut off the mouth of the balloon with scissors, then stretch the balloon over one end of the PVC.

3. Once the balloon is completely over the PVC section, feed the balloon back through the opening of the pipe. This will give the balloon more surface area with the pipe and prevent it from being pulled off when fired. If you like, you can add a zip tie over the stretched balloon to help secure it in place.

To fire, simply drop a small candy, such as an M&M, into the balloon, grip the PVC pipe, pull back the balloon, and release.

BATTERING RAM

MATERIALS AND TOOLS

- 3-FOOT LENGTH OF 2-INCH PVC PIPE
- TWO 4-INCH OR LARGER DRAWER PULLS
- MOUNTING HARDWARE
- DRILL AND BIT
- THIN PIECE OF WOOD APPROXIMATELY 12 INCHES LONG
- DOUBLE-SIDED TAPE
- SCREWDRIVER
- PVC CEMENT
- BAR CLAMP
- CONCRETE MIX
- PLASTIC BUCKET
- SMALL TROWEL
- TWO 2-INCH PVC ENDCAPS

You never know when the end days will rear its ugly head, so you might as well be prepared. A battering ram is a great tool for when the zombie apocalypse arrives and you need to break into a place or just crush some undead skulls. Either way, this cheap and easy project has you covered.

1. Though any large-diameter PVC pipe will work for this project, 2-inch PVC has a nice balance of size and heft. Place the drawer pulls along the PVC about 6 inches from each end and mark the mounting hole locations on the pipe, then drill the holes for the mounting hardware.

2. Insert the screws for the drawer pulls.

3. To place the nuts on the screws inside the pipe, use a thin strip of wood with a piece of double-sided tape on the end.

4

5

4. Place the nut on the tape and lower the stick into the pipe. Push the nut up against the screw and turn the screw to thread the nut and tighten. Repeat for all screws to fasten the handles to the pipe. Since you'll be filling the tube with concrete, it's not crucial to seat the nuts super tightly.

5. Use PVC cement to cap one end of the pipe.

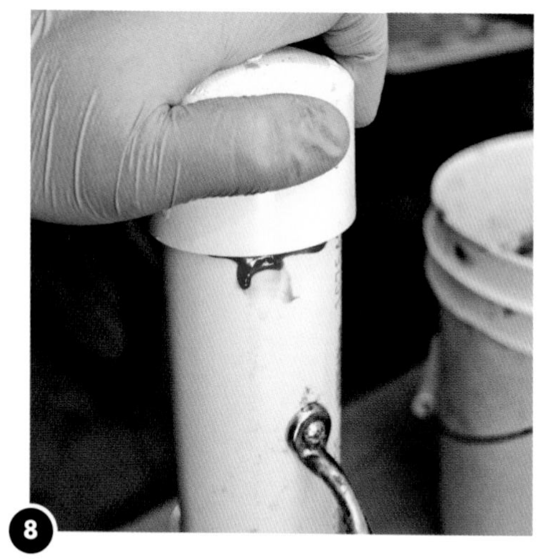

6. Stand the pipe upright with the opening facing upward and secure in place with a clamp.

7. Mix up a small batch of concrete and carefully fill the pipe to full, tapping the sides of the pipe as you go to remove air bubbles. A small amount of concrete should crest out the top. This will give the best ramming results.

8. Clean the end of the pipe, apply PVC cement, and cap the open ends of the pipe. Lay the pipe flat and allow the concrete to cure for 48 hours. Once the concrete has set, this battering ram is ready for action!

CO_2 MORTARS

MATERIALS AND TOOLS

- 4-FOOT LENGTH OF 3/4-INCH PVC PIPE
- 3/4-INCH PVC ENDCAP
- 1/2-INCH WOOD SCREW
- SCREWDRIVER
- CO_2 SELTZER-BOTTLE CARTRIDGES

NOTE: USE SCHEDULE 40 PVC

These incredibly dangerous projectiles are almost too easy to make, so be sure to only use them outside in a wide-open space where you—and others—are less likely to be struck by the scads of airborne cartridges sure to rain down from above.

1. Some quick measurements reveal that standard seltzer CO_2 cartridges fit almost perfectly inside ¾-inch PVC tubing, with just enough clearance to allow the cartridges to slide effortlessly up and down the tube.

2. To pierce the thin seal on the tapered end of the cartridges, which is what jettisons them from the tube, you will need to insert a small screw in the middle of the ¾-inch endcap. Drill a small pilot hole in the endcap and then insert the wood screw until about ¼ inch is exposed inside the cap.

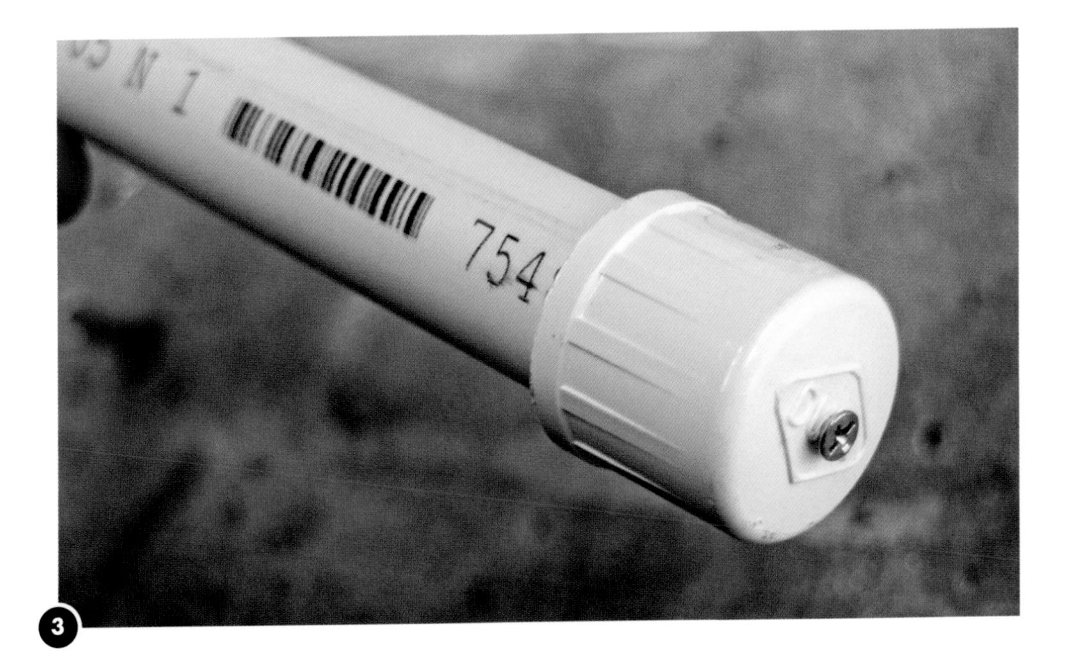

3

3. Place the endcap onto one end of the pipe and hand tighten until fully seated. This pipe is now the guideway that will fire the CO_2 projectiles.

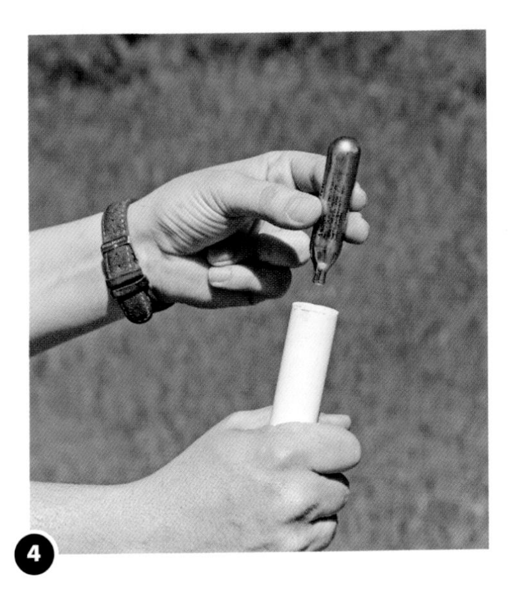

4

4. Drop a cartridge into the pipe with the tapered end facing down. When the cartridge hits the pointed end of the wood screw, it will expel the compressed gas. With nowhere to escape, the gas will send the cartridge up the tube and out the end of the pipe.

Remember: this project can be dangerous! Because there is loads of gas inside each of these small cartridges, they can reach very high speeds when shot from the barrel. It can't be stated enough that these small, fast-moving metal projectiles are basically bullets, so please treat them as such. Only fire these CO_2 mortars outside, in a clear and open area with no people or animals around.

TENNIS-BALL CANNON

MATERIALS AND TOOLS

- 1-INCH SOLENOID VALVE (USED IN AUTOMATIC SPRINKLER SYSTEMS)
- SCREWDRIVER
- DRILL WITH BITS AND HOLE SAW
- TWO-PART EPOXY
- 1/4-INCH BRASS STREET ELBOW
- 1/4-INCH BRASS NIPPLE
- TEFLON TAPE
- COMPRESSED-AIR DUSTER
- 24-INCH LENGTH OF 4-INCH PVC PIPE
- TWO 4-INCH PVC ENDCAPS
- TWO 1½-INCH PVC ELBOWS
- 12-INCH LENGTH OF 1½-INCH PVC PIPE (FOR CONNECTORS)
- 2-FOOT LENGTH OF 2½-INCH PVC PIPE (FOR BARREL—SEE BELOW FOR MORE DETAILS)
- TWO 1-INCH THREADED-TO-SLIP-FIT PVC ADAPTERS
- TWO 1½-TO-1-INCH REDUCING BUSHINGS
- PVC CEMENT
- THREADED PRESSURE GAUGE
- THREADED SCHRADER VALVE
- TENNIS BALLS

NOTE: USE SCHEDULE 40 PVC

There's something about the satisfying *thwomp* of launching a tennis ball that never gets old. Whether you're launching a ball for your dog or blasting your neighbor Doug for mowing his lawn too early, this launcher is something that will see a lot of use.

1. The most difficult part of this build is modifying the solenoid valve, so let's tackle that first. Almost all solenoid valves work the same way, so if yours doesn't look exactly like this one, don't worry. Start by removing the components on top of the solenoid—for mine, that meant the electronic switch and a small plug.

2. Next, remove the large screws holding the valve cap. Inside will be a large spring and a diaphragm. Be careful to keep these clean and undamaged.

3. Drill a new opening in the center of the valve top, directly over where the spring sits. Start with a small pilot hole, then expand the opening to fit the ¼-inch brass nipple. If you have access to a tap bit, this is a good application for it, but it's not necessary.

4. The small openings that formerly held the switch and small plug need to be filled with epoxy. Use a small dab on both sides of each opening to ensure they are filled and airtight. Set the cap aside for the epoxy to harden.

5. Wrap the brass street elbow and the brass nipple with Teflon tape.

6. Once the epoxy has hardened, attach the compressed-air duster to the brass elbow, then screw the duster-and-brass assembly into the new valve opening for an airtight fit.

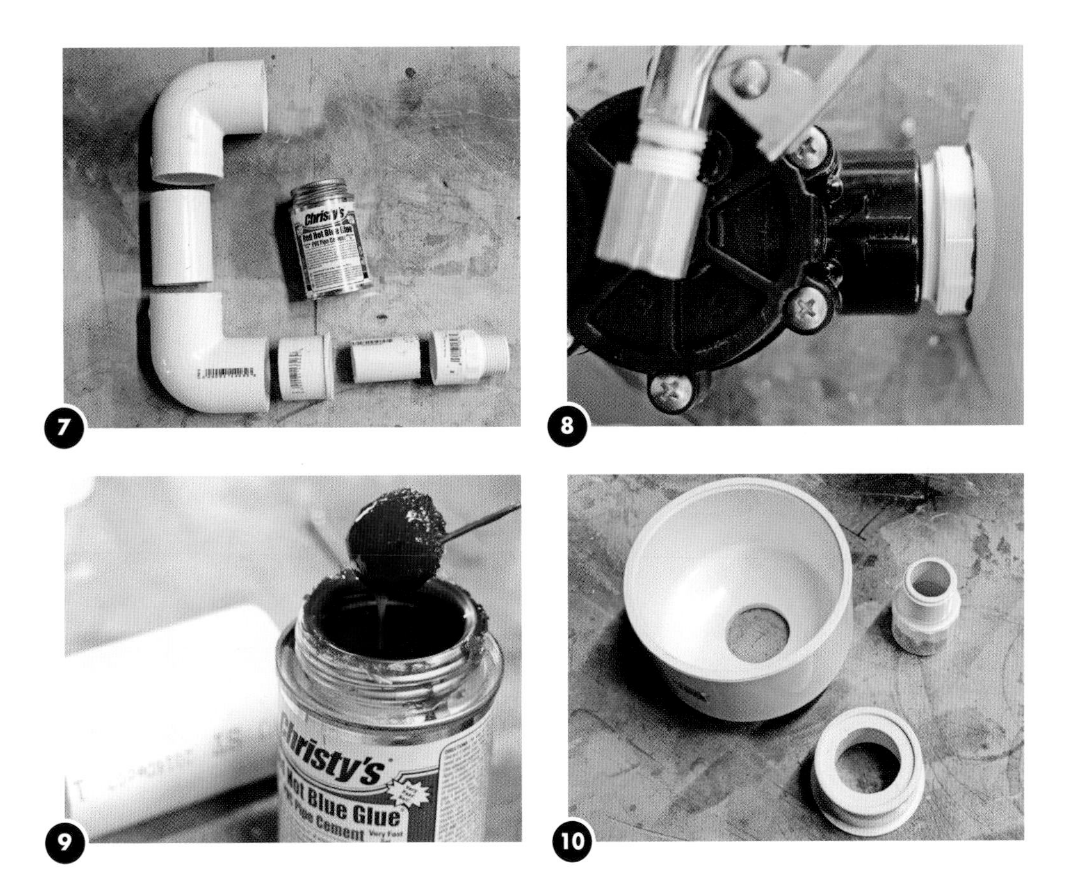

7. The solenoid valve I used has a 1-inch threaded opening on each end. I used a threaded-to-slip-fit adapter to join the valve to a reduction bushing using a 4-inch section of 1-inch pipe, which is then attached to two elbows.

8. This assembly is attached on the "exit" side of the valve. You can see a directional arrow on the valve indicating which way the flow should go.

9. The air reservoir is made from a 24-inch length of 4-inch PVC tube. Start by using PVC cement to affix a cap to one end.

10. There's no reduction bushing that goes from 4 inches to 1 inch, but we can make an adapter with a 1-inch threaded-to-slip connector and a 1½-inch-to-1-inch reduction bushing. These components sandwich the 4-inch PVC cap between them and make an airtight seal. Use a hole saw to drill an opening in the 4-inch PVC cap to match the outside diameter of the slip fitting. If you don't have a hole saw that matches the diameter, drill the closest undersized opening, then sand the opening until the connector fits.

11. Dry-fit the threaded-to-slip connector into the drilled opening and then place the reduction bushing from the other side to complete the connection. Use plenty of PVC cement to create this connection. Once the bond is made, seal the edges of each connection with epoxy to ensure airtight seals.

12. While the epoxy hardens, you can drill and install the pressure gauge and inflation valve. These can be located anywhere on the 4-inch PVC that makes sense with your design. Use more Teflon tape around the pressure gauge and inflation valve and component them into the holes you drilled.

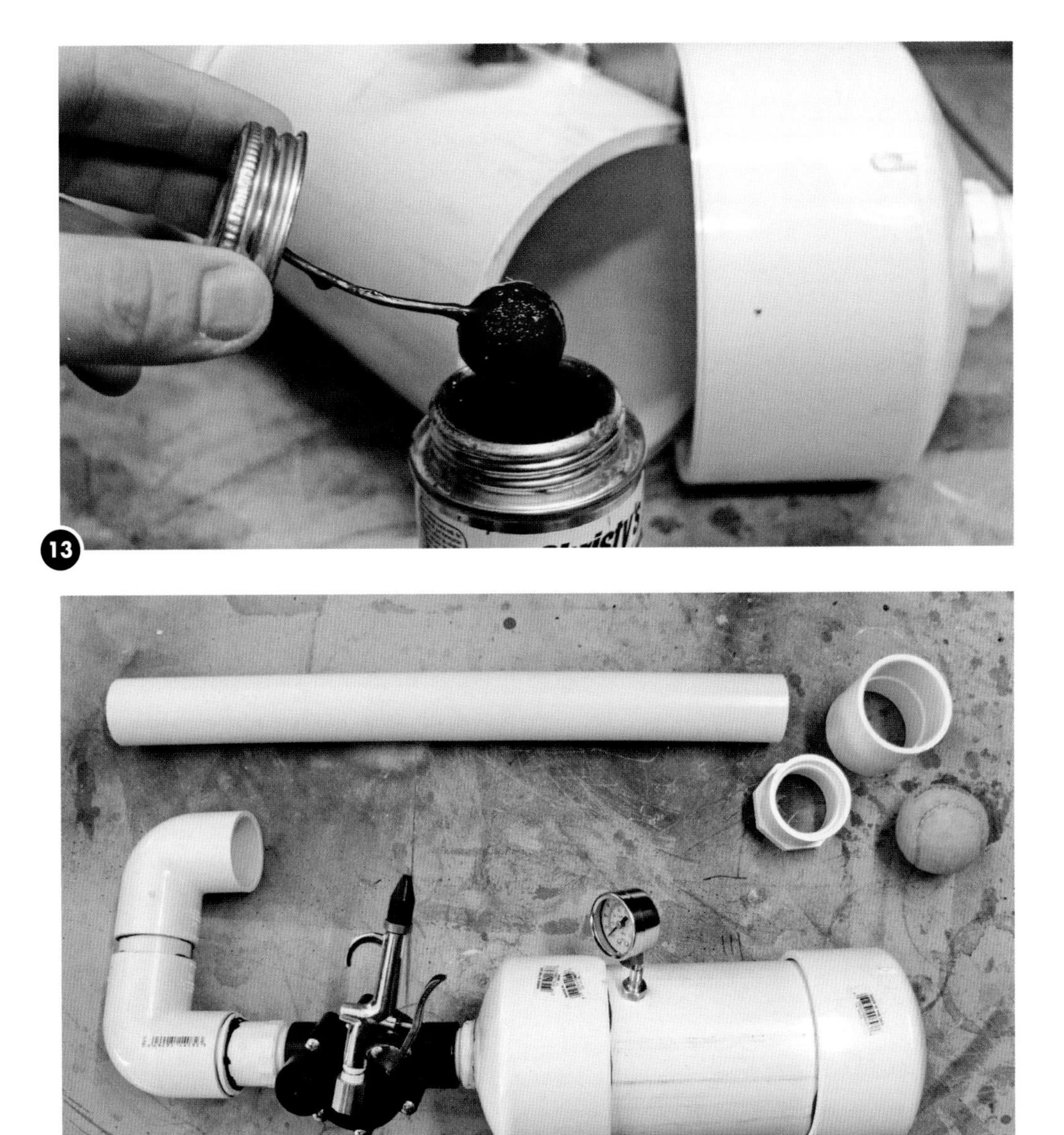

13. Use more PVC cement to attach the other 4-inch endcap.

14. While assembling the components, pay attention to the flow direction on the valve—it must flow from the 4-inch PVC tank toward the barrel.

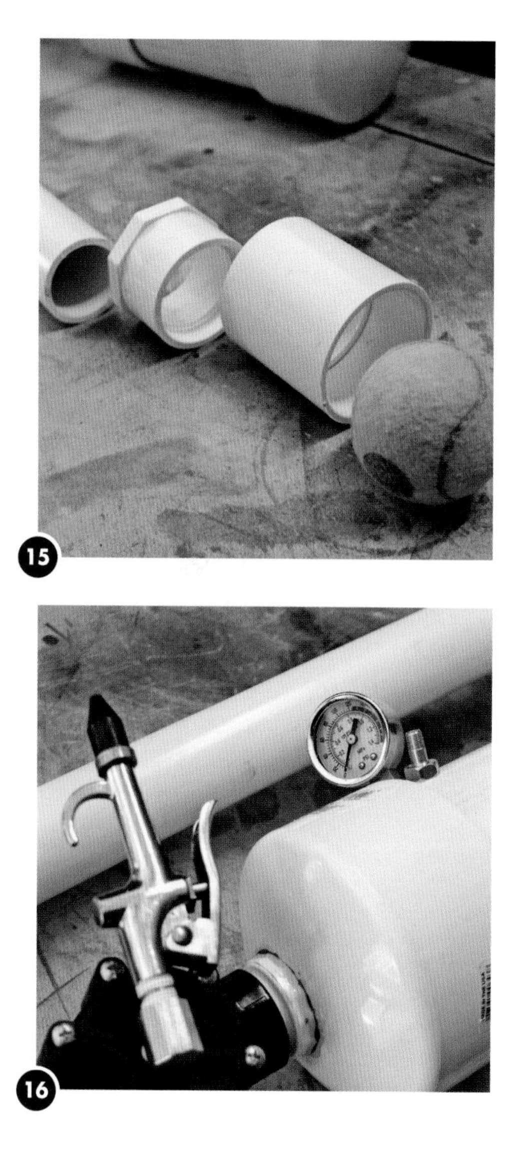

15. Tennis balls fit perfectly inside 2½-inch PVC, but that dimension is not commonly found in hardware stores. I chose a more readily available option that also fits a tennis ball: a 2-inch PVC coupling. Since a 2-inch PVC coupling goes over the outside of the pipe, it is actually larger than 2 inches in diameter, and thus can fit a tennis ball. From the top 1½-inch elbow, a 4-inch length of 1½-inch pipe is connected to a 1½-inch-to-2-inch reduction bushing. Then the 2-inch connector is attached to the reduction bushing. I left the barrel uncemented to allow me the option to change it up later if I ever find 2½-inch PVC pipe.

16. With all the components in place, the tank is ready for pressurization and testing for leaks. Start with 10 psi and listen for any leaks. Sudsy water spread over the joints can provide visual clues to any leaky spots. Use more PVC cement and epoxy to seal up any you find. The 4-inch Schedule 40 tank is rated for a maximum pressure of about 80 psi, so pay attention when filling it.

To fire your cannon, press the trigger of the air duster. The duster opens the valve and allows the pressure inside the tank to pass through, propelling the tennis ball.

TOOL CLIPS

MATERIALS AND TOOLS

- 1½-INCH PVC PIPE
- VISE
- SAW
- CLAMP
- HEAT GUN
- PLIERS
- DRILL AND BITS

I sometimes store all my long-handled tools bunched together and leaning in a corner. This storage solution might keep the brooms and shovels and rakes out of the way, but it's a mess when I try and get any one of them out. As it happens, it's super easy to make custom clips for long-handled tools out of PVC.

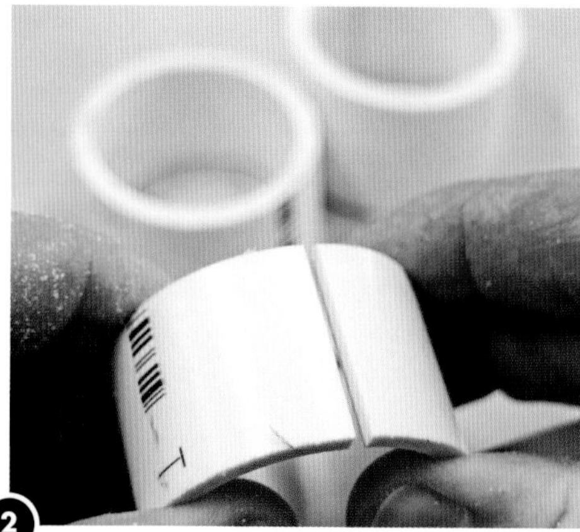

1. To start, I secured a length of 1½-inch PVC pipe in a bench vise and cut it into lengths of 1 to 1½ inches.

2. Cut a slit all the way down one side of each PVC section to open them up.

3. Clamp each split PVC length to the workbench with the slit facing up. Using a heat gun on low setting, warm up the PVC until it's pliable, then use pliers to uncurl the hot PVC from its ring shape.

4. Curl one end inward, then allow the PVC to cool while holding it in place with pliers or heat-resistant gloves until it's cool and keeps its shape. Repeat the process on the other side to create "rabbit ears." The tightness of the curl and the distance between curls will determine the springiness of your clip.

5. After the clip has cooled, test it out on a handle to ensure a good fit. Go back to the bench and adjust as necessary.

6. After making a few clips, drill a hole in the center of each to accept a mounting screw. Then simply attach the clips to your wall.

TOOL HOLDER

MATERIALS AND TOOLS

- **2-INCH, 45-DEGREE PVC ELBOWS**
- **SCRAP WOOD**
- **DRILL, ⅛-INCH BIT, AND PHILLIPS DRIVER BIT**
- **⅝-INCH WOOD SCREWS WITH WASHERS**

Staying organized in the shop is critical to staying productive, and keeping things in order doesn't need to break the bank. Next time you're in the hardware store, head over to the plumbing section and pick up two or three 2-inch or larger PVC elbows. I use the 45-degree elbows, but there's no rule as to what works best in your space.

1. Gather your PVC elbows and a suitable piece of scrap lumber for use as a backboard. The elbows will be mounted on the lumber, which will in turn distribute the weight along the wall where the holder is hung.

2. Space the elbows evenly along the backing.

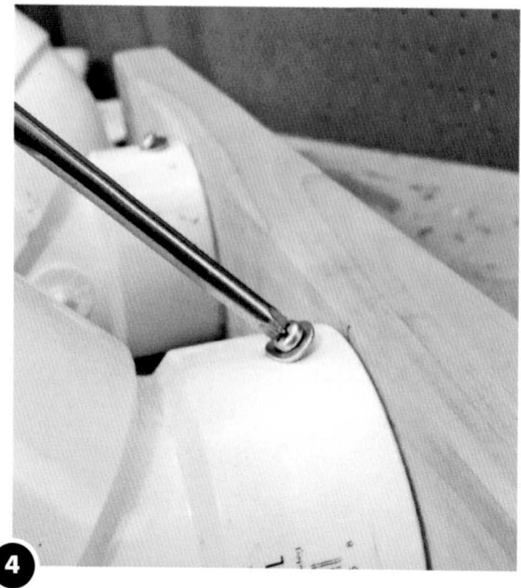

3. Drill a ⅛-inch opening through one end of each elbow on the inside of the bend. This is where the screw will attach the PVC to the wood backing.

4. Screw the elbows into place on the wood backing using one wood screw and washer for each.

5. The holder can now be mounted anywhere you need extra storage. Large hand tools can be placed inside the elbows and extension cords draped over each.

TOOL RACK

MATERIALS AND TOOLS

- 1–1½-INCH PVC PIPE
- SAW
- DRILL
- SCRAP WOOD
- ⅝-INCH WOOD SCREWS

Having your tools close at hand is the mark of an organized DIY and tinkerer. There are few storage solutions as flexible and easy to make than a PVC tool rack. These small sections of PVC pipe can accommodate a wide variety of tools, and you can always mix up the diameter of the pipe you use to make racks for all kinds of tools.

1. Start with any diameter of PVC pipe, and cut sections about 1 inch in length (longer if you think you have a specific tool that requires the additional length). No need to be too precise here if you don't want to be; your cuts don't need to be accurate to square.

2. Use a small-diameter drill bit to make an opening on one side of each cut length of pipe, then use a larger-diameter drill bit to make an opening on the opposite side of each length of pipe. The small opening is for a screw that will attach the pipe section to a wood frame, and the larger opening is to allow your screwdriver to drive the screw home from inside the pipe.

3. Position your cut lengths of PVC onto your scrap wood frame with the small opening facing the scrap wood. Use a short screw to secure the PVC sections to the scrap wood, passing the screwdriver through the large opening you drilled earlier.

4. The scrap wood can be attached to any solid surface. I have mine screwed into the stud behind my pegboard. A long screw can easily be passed between the sections of cut pipe on the scrap wood. The last step is to gather your pliers, scissors, or just about any other tool that doesn't fit neatly away somewhere, and start populating your PVC tool rack!

TOOL TROUGHS

MATERIALS AND TOOLS

- PVC PIPE (VARIOUS SIZES)
- RULER OR TAPE MEASURE
- PERMANENT MARKER
- SAW
- SANDPAPER

It doesn't matter what kind of maker you are—everyone has a drawer somewhere that's become a graveyard of loose items. Some call it a junk drawer. I call it a treasure-of-forgotten-items drawer, since you always seem to forget what's in there and are surprised when you find it.

The problem with most junk drawers is that it's usually oddly shaped things that get tossed in there. A good way to keep these loose items organized isn't with boxes but with troughs, which allow the irregular items to nest neatly up front without getting all jumbled up. PVC is a great material for this. You probably have some lying around, and you can use a variety of diameters as long as they're not too tall when cut in half to prevent the drawer from closing.

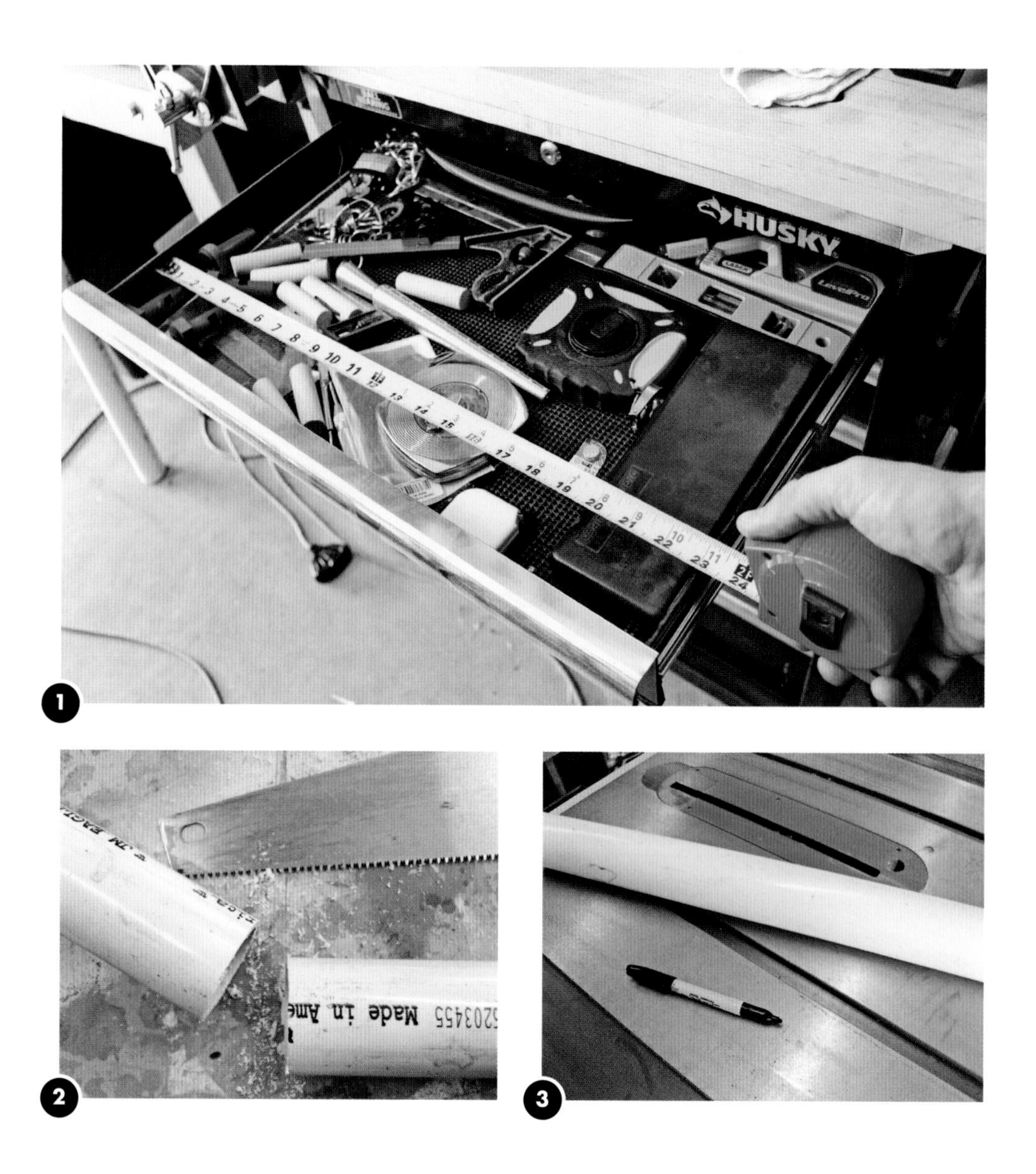

1. Measure the width of the drawer that needs some trough storage and make a mark on the PVC to match the length.

2. Cut the PVC to length.

3. To make a straight line along the PVC as your guide for cutting it lengthwise, a neat trick is to rest the PVC in a groove, like the miter track of a table saw or in a doorjamb. Rest a marker on the surface where the pipe is laid and run the marker down the length, making a perfectly straight line.

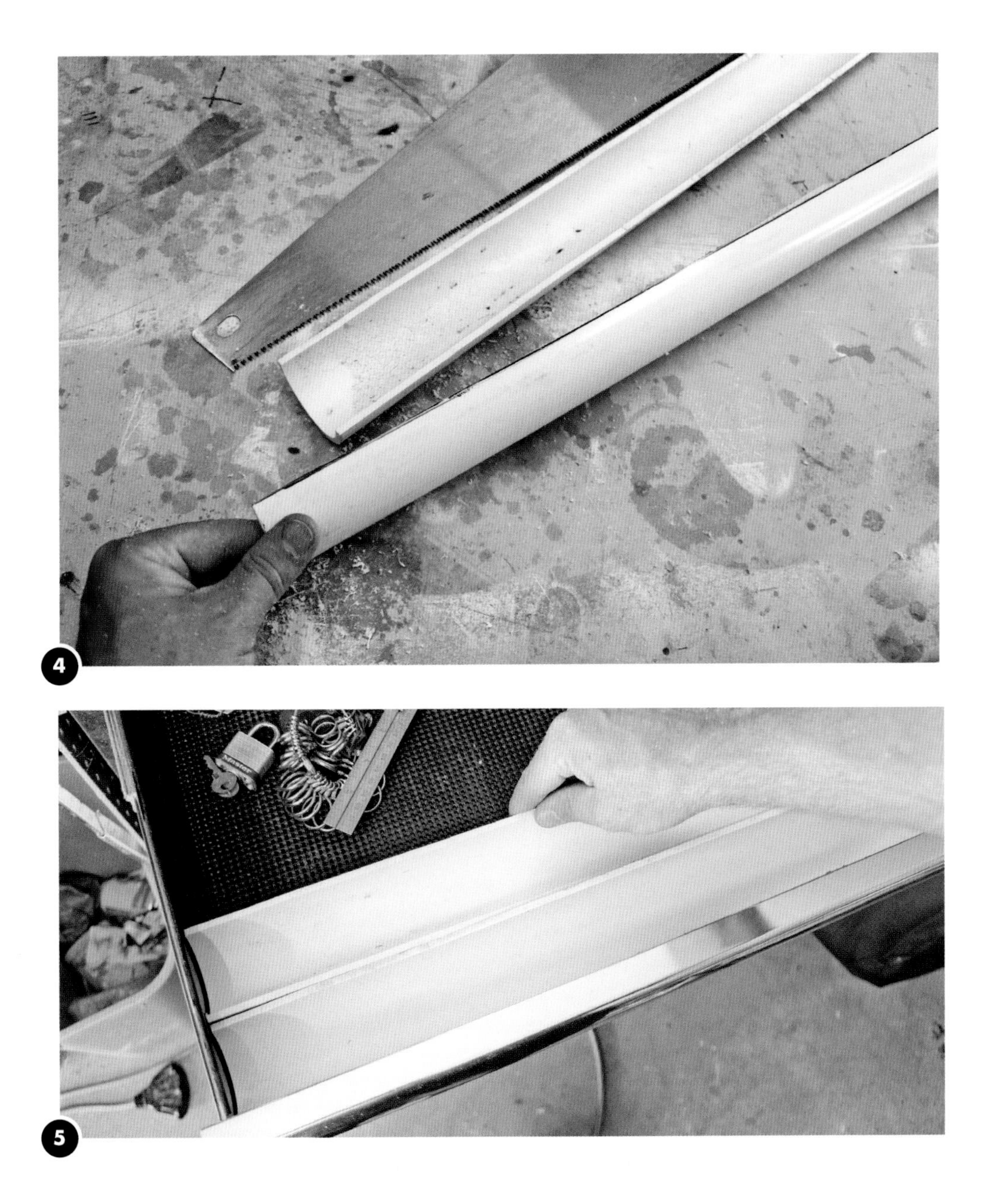

4. Cut the PVC pipe down its length to bisect it into two equal troughs. This cut can be done with just about any saw, as PVC is very soft. Clean up any plastic burrs with sandpaper for a nice smooth edge.

5. Clear out some space in your junk drawer and install the troughs, then fill with all your loose items to keep them organized, turning your eyesore into a yes drawer!

ACKNOWLEDGMENTS

I think sharing is a cornerstone of the maker community. This book would not have been possible without fearless creators: Creating personal projects and sharing their ideas, their failures, and their dreams with a wider audience, in order for others (and themselves) to grow. Making is a personal endeavor, but the results are always best when shared. It's a giant feedback loop. All of us are influenced by ideas and designs we've seen, but it's how we execute them that makes our creations unique.

I am humbled when my projects are remixed by others and shared, much the same way that I'm only passing on knowledge that I've accumulated over a lifetime of observing and prototyping.

We learn by doing, and we learn from one another. So this book is dedicated to every maker out there who's shared their successes, their failures, and their half-baked ideas for the world see and learn from. Thank you for doing what you do and being part of the best community of knowledge-sharers on earth.

ABOUT THE AUTHOR

Hello. I'm Mike, and I like to make stuff.

I'm a self-taught troublemaker, so this book speaks to me as the projects in these pages are the type of creations I made when I first got into making. Twenty years later, I'm a professional designer who builds functional prototypes out of whatever I can get my hands on. In all my designs I endeavor to explore the intersection of functionality with whimsical absurdity. My aim is to inspire, educate, and entertain. The results can be messy, but they are always fun!

My preposterous projects have been featured worldwide in print media like *Wired*, the *New York Times*, *Popular Science*, *C|NET*, and *New Scientist*. I've also had projects shown on *Jimmy Kimmel Live*, Daily Planet, Discovery, The Science Channel, and even on television in Japan, Canada, the United Kingdom, Iran, and Russia.

You can find more of my open source and photo-rich projects on Instructables or YouTube. I've also written a few books about making for kids: *23 Things to do Before You're 11½* and *The Gadget Inventor's Handbook*.

Happy making. :)